DATE DUE

D1295192

RHINOS

Endangered Species

MALCOLM PENNY

RHINOS
Endangered Species

MALCOLM PENNY

Facts On File Publications
New York, New York ● Oxford, England

First published in the United States of America by Facts On File, Inc.
460 Park Avenue South,
New York, New York 10016.

Library of Congress Cataloging-in-Publication Data

Penny, Malcolm.
    Rhinos: endangered species.

    1. Rhinoceros.   I. Title.
QL737.U63P46   1988   599.72'8   87–22360
ISBN 0-8160-1882-0

Printed in Great Britain

CONTENTS

COLOUR PLATES

FIGURES

FOREWORD

Malcolm Penny wrote this book in anticipation of my 1988 rhino crusade. The population of black rhinos is down to four or five hundred now; in the sixties we had 20,000. I shall be walking for the rhino again because it is our most endangered animal. The money raised will be donated to the existing rhino sanctuaries to buy fencing materials, boost up security, and pay for holding pens, translocation costs and the establishment of new protective zones. As on my previous walks I shall raise the money from individuals, companies and institutions, through sponsorship programmes.

Conservation cannot be imposed. It must have the understanding and support of the public, and especially those on whose land the animals live. So much of the conservation message has begun to sound sentimental and must seem horribly out of date to a man whose grain (his sole means of staying alive) has just been trampled by a herd of buffalo. We need to come up with practical solutions and systems in line with these realities and the present times: positive aims and positive actions. And surely the start of that is to know, really, what the problems are out there in the bush and among the farmers, out there at the grass roots.

On my walks I want to get people's views about what they feel about wildlife and current conservation measures. Their views will help me understand better what should be done to alleviate the tension created by the interaction between man and animal. My rhino campaign is only a symbol of conservation. If we don't save the rhino now how can we save the rest of the endangered species including the De Brazza monkey, Bongo antelope, Roan antelope and elephant? Like them, the rhino will live or die because of us.

Awareness of the rhino's plight is growing. Malcolm Penny's book will contribute further to our understanding of this animal and its perilous situation.

Michael Werikhe

Noted Kenyan rhino crusader Michael Werikhe has recently undertaken two sponsored walks in East Africa. In 1988 he is planning walks across the United States, and from Rome to London.

1
Introduction

Figure 1: The first and most famous illustration of a rhinoceros, by Albrecht Dürer. It gave rise to long-held misunderstandings about the toughness of its skin

'Nobody loves a rhinoceros much', sang Flanders and Swann on one of my favourite records. Of course, they went on to defend the beast, but their perception was true, as always. The Germans call the Indian rhinoceros *Panzernashorn*, the 'tank rhinoceros'; Dürer thought that it was held together with rivets, like a knight in armour, and made his famous drawing most explicitly impregnable. Ogden Nash announced that its hide could be penetrated only by platinum bullets; and an unfortunate private in the British Army during the Indian Mutiny was court-martialled for testing that belief a hundred years earlier by shooting the regimental mascot in a spirit of scientific enquiry.

After centuries of misunderstanding, there is a powerful movement today to defend the last of the world's great wild animals — the whales, tigers, bears and elephants — almost as if we have all come to realise, at the last minute before disaster, that unless we do something, now, there will be none left to inspire our descendants. The rhinoceroses have joined that doomed band of animals which has inspired the stubborn devotion of otherwise practical people. For some of these species, it might already be too late.

The fortunes of the black rhinoceros are declining so fast that the population figures given in this book will have fallen by the time you have finished reading it. The other four species, with one exception, are not much better off. The world is not ignoring the plight of the rhinoceroses: there are several schemes to help them. But in all of them, time is the crucial factor.

In the early 1960s, when the genetic code was just being unravelled, our lecturers at the University used to tell us that the best textbook for the foreseeable future would be *Scientific American*, with its month-by-month updates on the progress of research. A quarter of a century later, the genetic code is in every school biology syllabus, and the subjects on which there can be no definitive textbook have shifted to electronics, particle physics — and the state of the world's wildlife. And today, there are numerous official, semi-official and amateur conservation bodies which can keep us up to date.

The journals of the august scientific societies chronicle the research which produces the results, but for the results themselves we would do better to turn, for example, to the quarterly *Traffic Bulletin*, published by the Wildlife Trade Monitoring Unit of the International Union for the Conservation of Nature. Alternatively, the pages of *Oryx*, the journal of the Fauna and Flora Preservation Society, give regular reports from around the world.

A source which is even more up to date is the admirable nature coverage in certain national daily newspapers, such as the *Daily Telegraph* or the *Guardian* in Britain. Both give regular bulletins on the world's threatened populations of animals. Television has played a large part in creating and encouraging a heightened public awareness of the plight of endangered wild animals, but it takes time to get programmes on to the screen. The press has developed and followed this awareness, usually overtaking television with the most recent information.

Why, then, write a book about rhinoceroses, when some at least of the information in it will be out of date by the time it has gone through the presses? There are several reasons, which I shall summarise here, in the hope that they will become more apparent in the course of the book itself.

First, four out of the five species of rhinoceroses in the world are in real danger of becoming extinct before the end of this century. The single exception is the white rhinoceros in South Africa. That species reached its nadir in the 1930s, but it is now recovering from its lowest ebb after heroic and determined management, and is secure for the foreseeable future. The Javan and Sumatran rhinoceroses are virtually extinct, though the remainder are being protected in tiny remnants of their habitat. The Indian one-horned rhinoceros is making a last stand in very limited areas of southern Nepal and northern India. The African black rhinoceros has suddenly come under a sustained attack, financed from outside its home countries, which threatens to extinguish it in all of Africa north of the Limpopo River, though the front line of the fierce fight to save it lies at present at the Zambesi River.

Second, the reasons for the apparently unstoppable plunder of rhinoceros populations, particularly that of the black rhinoceros, are not always clearly understood. It is not, as we read so often in the newspapers, simply a matter of supplying a number of elderly Chinese with their daily aphrodisiac, nor of supplying a few Arabs with some fancy knives. If it were, I doubt whether the death toll among poachers would be so high. Forty-three invading poachers from Zambia were shot in the first three months of 1987, crossing the Zambesi to hunt black rhinoceroses in northern Zimbabwe. The medical uses of rhinoceros horn are many, and very deeply embedded in the culture of the Chinese and Japanese peoples. Similarly, there is much more to a *jambia* dagger than a fancy knife to stick into one's belt: if there were not, the men of the Yemeni Republic would not be willing to pay as much as $30,000 for one.

Misunderstanding the trade in rhinoceros horn, whether for medical uses or for ornamental dagger-handles, can lead to a serious underestimation of its importance to certain groups of people, the Chinese in particular. Although they are otherwise law-abiding and humane, they will not be deprived of their traditional remedial medicines without a long and difficult period of persuasion. If the rhinoceroses are to survive into the next century, some way will have to be found of controlling the medicinal trade in horns, hooves and skin, to stem its destructive effect on rhinoceros populations. Force, whether physical or political, will be of no avail.

Third, there are many organisations around the world which are successfully collecting money for charities whose aim is to save rhinoceroses. Many, if not most, of their benefactors are people who have never seen a wild rhinoceros in their lives. The charities often seem to be extracting the money with arguments and emotional pleas which create a false impression in their hearers. This is not to accuse the collection agencies themselves of dishonesty — far from it — but merely to remark that the quality of seed is immaterial if it falls on stony ground, or into a lake of misunderstanding.

The fourth and perhaps the most powerful reason arises from a recent conversation in London.

A devoted fund-raiser for wildlife projects all over the world was discussing the success of his efforts to raise money to save the black rhinoceros. Thousands of pounds have been collected already, at an early stage of the project. When I asked him what the money was to be spent on, he told me that they were going to buy radio sets, so that game rangers could keep more closely in touch with each other, and electric fences and rifles with which they could defend the animals in their charge. He seemed very surprised when I suggested to him that what he and his colleagues were really doing was buying arms to be used in a bush war.

It is a sad fact that most rural Africans are rather fond of poachers: poachers give them money and food in exchange for small services such as showing them where the rhinoceroses are to be found. They rather dislike rhinoceroses, which are a nuisance and can be dangerous: and they positively hate game rangers, who prevent their dealing with either poachers or rhinoceroses in the way which they would prefer. In the event of an out-and-out fight over who will have control over the lands from which the rhinoceroses are presently being poached, there is little doubt that the local farmers and smallholders will take the side of the poachers. When they need weapons, they will be supplied — from the poachers' substantial armoury. My good friend is providing the finance which will arm the rangers in their attempt to take the upper hand by force, and he is just as surely compelling the rural Africans to accept the offered Kalashnikovs next time they meet the poachers.

This book would not be complete without a summary of the facts about each species of rhinoceros, as far as they are known. In the case of the Javan and Sumatran rhinoceroses that is not very far, but such information as there is here. However, the main purposes of the book are to describe and explain the trade in parts of dead rhinoceroses, and why it is so important to those who engage in it; to explain some recent theories about conservation; and to try to prevent my friend and his supporters from financing a bush war.

I hope very much that not all of my readers are converted, yet. I should like to think that there is someone reading this page who is asking why the black rhinoceros, or any other, should be saved. I reply that there are several reasons, three of which I give here:

1   Allowing any species to become extinct from preventable causes is a symptom of disregard for the natural environment which can only end in disaster for the human race.
2   The survival of any ecosystem depends on all its members, large or small, beautiful or ugly, valuable or worthless to humanity.
3   Rhinoceroses are, as I shall hope to show, interesting, awe-inspiring, peaceable — in short, nice animals and well worth saving.

2
The Evolution of Rhinoceroses

Imagine meeting an animal 20 ft (6 m) tall at the shoulder and 23 ft (7 m) long, with a head nearly $6\frac{1}{2}$ ft (2 m) long at the end of a powerful, horse-like neck. Its feet, if you took the time to glance down at them, would have had three toes each, and the fact that the animal was herbivorous would have been small comfort in the wide open spaces of the Mongolian plains. Its defensive armoury consisted not of horns, but of two sharp tusks, formed from the incisors of its lower jaw. *Indricotherium*, the name given by palaeontologists to this huge hornless browsing rhinoceros, became extinct about ten million years ago. It represented the peak of rhinoceros evolution, at a time when the group as a whole was very successful both in the Old World and the New.

In evolutionary terms, rhinoceroses are the surviving members of one branch of a very ancient line of animals, the ungulates, which were the first mammals to develop hooves. Their ancestors included the paenungulates, or 'nearly-hooved' animals, and the protungulates, or 'first hooved' animals, both long extinct.

Rhinoceroses belong to the group known as the perissodactyls, or 'odd-toed ungulates', which includes horses and tapirs. The group originated in the Eocene Period, about 50 million years ago. In the following 40 million years, leading up to the Pliocene and Pleistocene Periods, the perissodactyls were themselves replaced to a large extent by the modern artiodactyls, the 'even-toed ungulates', including deer, gazelles and antelopes, as well as pigs, camels and hippopotamuses. The artiodactyls also arose in the Eocene Period, but they evolved along a different course before finally gaining the advantage over the perissodactyls. They became fast movers, with keen senses and well-developed brains, and efficient grinding and cropping teeth. Most important of all, many of them became ruminants, with stomachs which enabled them to digest cellulose by fermenting it with the aid of bacteria.

The slow-moving, slow-witted and somewhat dyspeptic perissodactyls represent an ancient line most of whose members are coming to the end of their evolutionary career. The exception is their relatives the horses, some of which are still very successful, even the wild species which lack the intervention of humans in their breeding and feeding.

Although all five surviving species of rhinoceros look rather similar, and are descended from a remote single common ancestor, they are the modern ends of two evolutionary lines which diverged about 30 million years ago, in the middle of the Oligocene. One line led to the one-horned rhinoceroses, represented today by the rather primitive, forest-dwelling Javan rhinoceros and the more advanced grazing Indian species. The other line gave rise to the two-horned species, one branch of it by way of the woolly rhinoceros, which survived into the Stone Age — the Sumatran rhinoceros is its only surviving direct descendant. About ten million years ago, a branch of the two-horned group found its way into Africa, where it set off along the evolutionary road which led to today's black and white rhinoceroses. They evolved to feed without cutting teeth, and therefore lost the incisors which form the tusks of the other species. Their horns became their main defensive weapons, being longer and sharper than those of their Asian relatives.

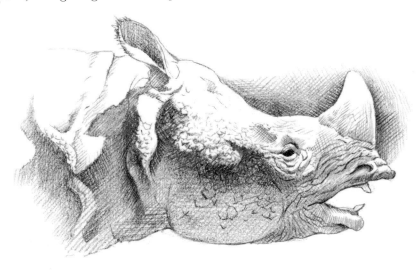

Figure 2: The Indian rhinoceros, like all the Asian species, retains its incisors, and occasionally uses them as weapons

The surviving species are a tiny remnant of the vast and varied range of animals which lived during the heyday of the rhinoceroses. The fossil record is surprisingly full. The extinct species took a number of different forms, many of them quite unlike modern rhinoceroses. Forty or 50 million years ago, in the Eocene, their relationship to horses was much clearer, in the long-limbed species of the families Hyrachidae and Hydracodontidae, whose fossils are found in North America. These 'running rhinoceroses' already had three toes on each foot, an arrangement also found in the horses of the period. There is evidence that the Hyrachidae were technically the very first rhinoceroses; but their descendants explored many evolutionary blind alleys before they arrived at the forms which we know today.

Also in North America, as well as in Eurasia, there were tubby, hippopotamus-like creatures, the Amynodonts, or 'defensive-toothed' rhinoceroses, which were partly aquatic, and more like the modern animal in appearance. The oldest rhinoceroses which we would recognise as such, the Caenopenes and the Aceratheres, appeared about 30 million years ago in the Oligocene in North America and Europe. They were distinctly rhinoceros-shaped, but their fossil skeletons show no sign of horns. They have a complete dentition, not the specialised grinding equipment which was to develop later, with little or no distinction between molar and premolar teeth. Just before they died out, in the Pliocene, they had begun to develop small horns, but their principal weapons of defence still seem to have been the lower incisors, which had developed into considerable tusks. The name Aceratheres means 'hornless animals'.

Their close relatives, the Paraceratheres, produced some of the biggest rhinoceroses, which were also the largest terrestrial mammals ever to have lived. They occurred in Eurasia during the first three ages of the Tertiary, the Eocene to the Miocene, usually dated between 60 and 10 million years ago. The biggest of the group, which we met at the beginning of this chapter, was *Indricotherium asiaticum*. Its fossil remains, found in Kazakhstan in central Russia, were dated at 35 million years old. A very similar animal, found in the Gobi Desert in the early 1920s, was *Paraceratherium*, which had no horns but formidable tusks. Its low-crowned molars reveal it to have been a browser, with a reach not much less than that of a modern giraffe.

The great Indian rhinoceros, *Rhinoceros unicornis*, and the Javan rhinoceros, *Rhinoceros sondaicus*, are descended from the line which included the Caenopenes, themselves descended from the long-legged running rhinoceroses of the Eocene. The Javan is the older species: it can be found in its present form in fossil deposits more than a million years old.

Asiatic two-horned rhinoceroses appeared in the Miocene, 15 million years ago. One of their descendants was the woolly rhinoceros, *Coelodonta antiquitatis*, which was first discovered in 1799 in the permafrost of Siberia, complete with skin and fur. Drawings of this species occur in the cave paintings of the early Stone Age, but it was extinct by the end of the last Ice Age, 15,000 years ago. Although frozen specimens have been found with willow leaves and fragments of coniferous twigs between their teeth, it seems to have been principally a grass-eating species. Its dentition was very similar to that of the modern white rhinoceros, with no front teeth and high-crowned molars suitable for grinding the tough, silicaceous grasses of the Steppes. However, this merely shows that the two species evolved to eat similar diets, and says nothing about their true relationship to each other. It is an example of 'convergent evolution'.

Forest rhinoceroses survived into the Ice Ages as well, including one species with a close resemblance to the modern Sumatran rhinoceros, *Dicerorhinus sumatrensis*, with front teeth and low-crowned molars suitable for eating forest vegetation rather than grass. In fact, the Sumatran rhinoceros has been said to be a survivor, almost unmodified, from the Tertiary Period. It is certainly the most primitive form of the family alive today.

The two African species, the black rhinoceros, *Diceros bicornis* and the white or square-lipped rhinoceros, *Ceratotherium simum*, are a separate branch of the family which split from the Asiatic two-horned rhinoceroses around the end of the Miocene, 10 million years ago. The black is thought to be the more primitive species, a browser from which the grazing white rhinoceros separated between four

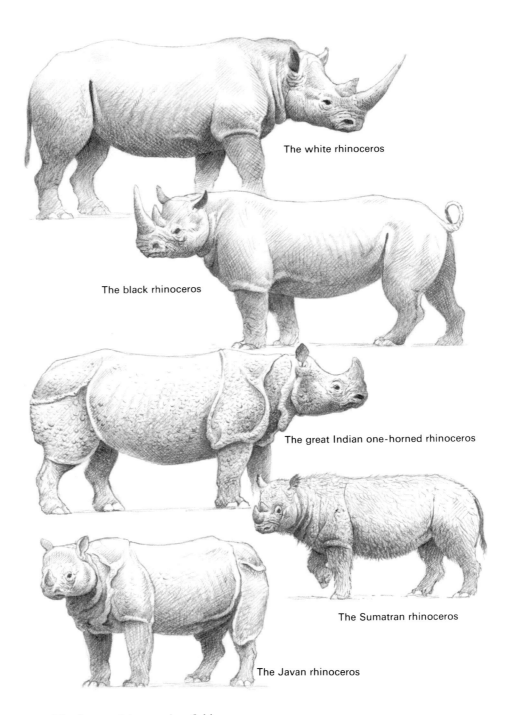

The white rhinoceros

The black rhinoceros

The great Indian one-horned rhinoceros

The Sumatran rhinoceros

The Javan rhinoceros

Figure 3: The five surviving species of rhinoceros

and five million years ago. The two species are still closely enough related for some taxonomists to doubt whether they should be separated into two genera.

The Last of Their Line

Rhinoceroses are an example of a major animal group which is long past the peak of its evolutionary development. Their heyday was 40 million years ago, when massive animals like *Indricotherium* and *Paraceratherium* roamed the plains of Mongolia, and lithe runners and sub-aquatic wallowers occupied niches away from the woodlands where the giant browsers lived.

Opinions differ about the reason for the decline of these huge animals: they must have been ponderous in motion, their weight poised over their front limbs, counter-balanced by their massive heads. Because of their size, they are unlikely to have been the victim of any contemporary predator. One suggestion is that a major change took place in the vegetation of their principal range, which at one time was the forest zone stretching across Eurasia from the British Isles to India. They had low-crowned molars, suggesting that they were browsers not grazers; if the woodlands had given way to steppe or savannah, where grass was the principal or only food available, they would have been at a severe disadvantage. The Sumatran rhinoceros might be considered to be the only true descendant of the old browsing rhinoceroses, the others having evolved to eat grass, or perished.

The slow movement and generally placid demeanour of rhinoceroses must have made them very easy to hunt. Cave paintings at Font-de-Gaume and other sites in France indicate that Stone Age man was familiar with the woolly rhinoceros, and almost certainly hunted it. At the end of the last century, hunters in Sumatra used sharpened stakes in pits dug in the rhinoceroses' habitual trails as a means of killing their local species. African tribesmen, before the advent of guns, used similar weapons and presumably similar hunting methods. They would have been capable of killing rhinoceroses from an early time. However, when white explorers and hunters first penetrated the interior of southern Africa, in the second half of the nineteenth century, both species of rhinoceros were plentiful, with no sign that they had been under any particular hunting pressure from the local people. Frederick Courtney Selous, the first of the great white hunters, whose first major expedition was in 1873, blamed European hunters for the decline of both species during the following 20 years.

Although it is tempting to place the blame for the decline of the surviving rhinoceros species entirely on the hunting activities of humans, there are other factors which ought to be borne in mind. The preparation of land in East Africa for agricultural settlement after the Second World War caused the death of very large numbers. Bernhard Grzimek, the great German naturalist, mentions in his *Animal Life Encyclopaedia*, the British hunter, John A. Hunter, who killed 300 rhinoceroses in 1947 and 500 in the following year, in the course of government-sponsored clearance work for African farming settlements. In India, in Assam especially, the clearing of land for tea plantations was a principal cause of the decline of the Indian species. Even without the direct killing, the clearance of woodland and scrub would have been similar in its effect to the hypothetical change in vegetation which might have accounted for the decline of the large browsing species of the Oligocene.

Clearing for rubber plantations had the same effect on the Sumatran rhinoceros in Malaysia. Many animals were shot, but the removal of their feeding grounds and breeding territories was surely as serious a blow to their populations.

The Swiss zoologist, Ernst Lang, sums up the position of the modern rhinoceroses thus:

> Compared to this multitude of forms in the Tertiary and glacial rhinoceros, the surviving four genera seem rather stunted in spite of their size. They all live in remote habitats, seemingly because they have not been able to compete any longer with the other ungulates, especially the ruminants. Above all, however, human influence has basically changed wide areas of Asia and Africa, thus making them uninhabitable for rhinoceros.

Adult rhinoceroses have very few predators, though there are recorded cases of lions and even a crocodile killing them. Grzimek relates a most unusual account of a rhinoceros being torn to pieces by a hippopotamus, which surfaced as the rhinoceros was about to drink from a pool. However, it is unlikely that predation was the cause of the extinction of any of the earlier species. It is true now, though, that the presence of spotted hyaenas has a serious effect on the recruitment rate, or population growth rate, of the slow-breeding black rhinoceros.

Humanity cannot prevent the eventual extinction of the rhinoceroses. It is inevitable in geological time, and is in fact going on around us now, as it has been for many million years. The perissodactyls are an outmoded group, incapable of competing on equal terms with the artiodactyls, for all that they are safer from predation. What we can do is to ensure that we reduce the pressure on them from our own species, so that they can become extinct, not in the geological second represented by our brief appearance as a destructive force, but in the natural course of events, many thousands of years from now.

3
The Life of a Rhinoceros

The life of a rhinoceros is dominated by the fact that it is an ungulate. The ungulates are all herbivores, that is to say primary consumers. Their somewhat thankless ecological role is to act as a channel for energy passing from plants to carnivores: they are the primary food source of most large predators. In the past, rhinoceroses were probably also prey animals — food for such as the now extinct sabre-tooth tiger — today, although they are rarely taken as prey, rhinoceroses still retain other characteristics of the ungulates. Ungulates are usually shy, retiring animals. Their weapons are defensive rather than offensive, and they are alert to sights, scents and sounds which indicate the approach of danger. Their principal reaction to a threat is to run rather than to stand and fight.

In all of these respects, rhinoceroses are typical ungulates. They are also typical perissodactyls. Because they are large and sturdy, they do not need to be able to run as fast as their relatives the horses: instead, they have developed a thick skin which can withstand an attack should it be unavoidable.

Rhinoceroses are not gregarious. Their size and their digestive apparatus affect their feeding behaviour, so that it is inefficient for them to feed in sociable herds. Their digestion is slow, so that their food intake must be bulky and reliable. The cellulose in their diet is broken down by bacterial action, not in the stomach, as in artiodactyls, but in the caecum, an arrangement which enables them to tolerate large quantities of fibre. Their food requirements are such that an individual needs a home range where it can feed alone, moving slowly around a limited area from which others are excluded, or in which they are tolerated but not welcomed. There is no direct correlation between the amount of food available and the animal's size, but big rhinoceroses may be able to win access to more food than their smaller neighbours, dominating them and thus enlarging their own territories by ritualised conflicts in which the heavier animal will always be the winner.

Rhinoceroses need regular access to water. Most of them have to drink daily, though during droughts the two African species can manage three or four days without water. Rhinoceroses cannot sweat, so they also need water or mud as a means of keeping cool by wallowing. A large body tends to overheat, and having a small surface area relative to its volume it needs some assistance in cooling down: mud is an excellent way of accelerating heat loss, taking over an hour to dry, and absorbing heat from the body in the process. Rhinoceroses have developed behaviour which takes full advantage of this, and also of the therapeutic properties of mud for maintaining the skin in a healthy condition. A thick coating of mud probably serves also to reduce the attentions of biting flies and to protect the rhinoceros from other parasites. Ticks and lice tend to fall off with the mud when it dries. Access to water may well be the crucial factor determining how many rhinoceroses can live in a particular area.

Figure 4: Wallowing is an important part of the daily routine, for keeping cool, protection against parasites, and keeping the skin supple

Senses

The sense of smell of a rhinoceros is very acute: the volume of its nasal passages is actually greater than that of its brain. Scent is important as a means of detecting danger at a distance, to give the rhinoceros time to prepare its escape: but such sensitivity has other uses. Rhinoceroses have evolved a pattern of behaviour in which scent is the principal means of signalling to others of their kind. Urine and dung are obviously important in this system of communication, but so too are flakes of skin, which may be left on trees which are used as regular rubbing posts, or on bushes as the rhinoceros brushes past. Dried mud which falls from the skin between wallows probably serves the same purpose, carrying the scent of its erstwhile wearer. The territory of a dominant male rhinoceros is labelled all over with invisible scent-markers of this kind. Round the boundaries are dung-heaps and urine-sprayed bushes whose significance we will consider later.

Their hearing, too, is acute, with large swivelling ears to locate the direction of suspicious sounds: another typical adaptation of an animal which, contrary to appearances, is descended from a long line of prey animals.

The vision of rhinoceroses, however, is not very good, though they are not half-blind, as people used to think. They are short-sighted, apparently able to perceive movement but not detail beyond a range of about 100 ft (30 m). This may be a reflection of their evolutionary history as forest dwellers: the only species which is ever likely to be confronted with a wide vista in its natural habitat is the white rhinoceros of the open African plains, which is usually considered to be very advanced in evolutionary terms.

There has been some discussion about whether rhinoceroses have binocular or stereoscopic, 3-D vision. A common adaptation of prey animals is to sacrifice stereoscopy for a wide-angle view. Accounts by early hunters, such as Selous, often contain descriptions of a rhinoceros looking at its pursuers first with one eye and then the other, like some huge bird, suggesting that it does not have binocular vision. However, such accounts may well have been mistaken: as Jonathan Kingdon, the East African zoologist, has pointed out, a common display between two challenging males is 'head-flagging'. When two rival males meet, whilst they are still some way apart, they turn their heads from side to side — possibly to demonstrate the size of their horns. This might be a symbolic, long-distance version of the horn-wrestling which occurs when the animals are within reach of each other. He gives sketches in which both eyes are clearly visible from the front when the animal's head is in its normal feeding position, suggesting that in spite of the obstruction presented by its large nose, surmounted by a horn, a rhinoceros does have binocular vision, at least over a limited field. The hunters were probably being challenged by a gesture in rhinocerosese rather than merely being inspected.

The stiff-legged, strutting walk which is seen in some displays would also be of little use if the rhinoceros were really half-blind. This, together with the head-flagging display, suggests that at close enough range rhinoceroses can see perfectly well.

A Ponderous Tread

From their build, rhinoceroses look as though they should move slowly and ponderously. Their pillar-like legs and huge head seem to be designed for standing still, rather than moving at all. The form of their body is very similar to that of their distant, heavyweight, and extinct, ancestors. The vertebrae have long spines for the attachment of muscles which support the back and the weight of the head. The head itself acts as a counter-balance, so that the whole body pivots over the front legs. The main pelvic bones, the ilia, are nearly vertical and the rhinoceros has more ribs than other perissodactyls: these are both adaptations for carrying great body weight.

The basic number of toes in mammals is five. Modern rhinoceroses have three on each foot, in contrast to the swift-running artiodactyls, which have two. The middle digit takes the weight of the animal, rather than the axis passing between the second and third, as in the artiodactyls. It is this which sets the perissodactyls, the tapirs, horses and rhinoceroses, apart from the artiodactyls, the even-toed ungulates. Even when they had four toes on the fore feet, the extinct rhinoceroses took their weight on the third digit: hence 'odd-toed'. The three toes produce the typical 'ace of clubs' footprint, showing that rhinoceroses support their weight on a

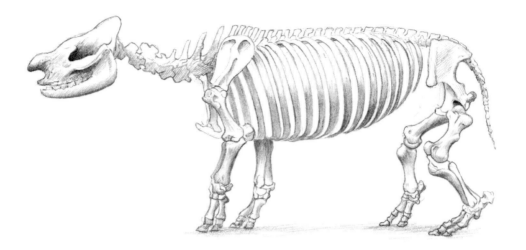

Figure 5: The skeleton of a black rhinoceros is typical of all species, having large attachments for the muscles which support the head, and numerous ribs

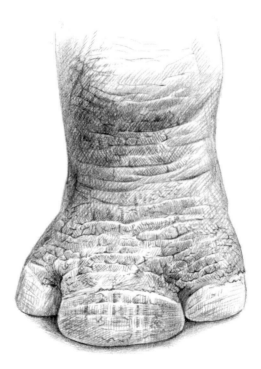

Figure 6: Black rhinoceros forefoot. The toes are reduced to three in all species, the middle digit taking the weight of the animal

relatively large area, most of it on the front legs. The thrust when the animal moves comes mainly from the hind legs.

As many have remarked, this weighty and clumsy-looking creature is capable of moving quite swiftly when the need arises. Kingdon has stated that the black rhinoceros can charge at up to 31 miles (50 km) per hour, and that it is very manoeuvrable. Selous, extracts from whose diary will appear in more detail later, had great respect for the speed and stamina of rhinoceroses. One female, into which he had fired two bullets, trotted off 'as fast as an eland . . . it is very little use following either elephants or rhinoceroses, however desperately they may have been wounded, unless, indeed, one of their legs has been injured'. He found many times that they 'walk on and on until they drop', and was amazed that these 'unwieldy-looking beasts run at a pace that, with their short legs and heavy bodies, one would not believe them capable of'.

Teeth and Feeding

The feeding mechanism of perissodactyls such as the rhinoceroses is generally less specialised than that of artiodactyls. Originally, they all had incisors, which they used for cropping grass and leaves. These teeth had a hollow on the outside surface, which meant that as they were worn away they remained sharp. Both African species have now lost their front teeth, though the Asian species retain them. The canines, if they are present at all, are usually much reduced; but the primitive Sumatran rhinoceros has well-developed lower canines, which it can use as tusks for fighting rather than for food-gathering.

The grinding teeth of the early perissodactyls were at first low-crowned, suitable for eating leaves but not silicaceous grasses. Later, horses and some rhinoceroses developed high-crowned molars which enabled them to eat grass. Modern rhinoceroses are therefore able to make use of a fairly broad diet: a feature which may well be the main reason for their survival.

Animals which are too specialised in their feeding preferences die out when there are changes to the food available to them. Such a change may be the result of an alteration in climate, or an increase in some other species with which the specialists are unable to compete. One of the signs which enable palaeontologists to state for certain when the true rhinoceroses appeared in the fossil record is the elaboration of the grinding teeth: a true rhinoceros has no recognisable premolars, but instead a long row of fully-developed molars, sometimes referred to as 'molarised premolars'.

The specialist feeders among the profusion of ancient rhinoceroses were the first to succumb to the changes in vegetation, which whittled the surviving species down to the present five. Although the Javan and Sumatran rhinoceroses are both almost entirely browsers, occasionally even breaking down small trees to get at the leaves in their crowns, both will also take fruit, as does the African black rhinoceros. The Indian one-horned rhinoceros is a grazer, but it can make use of its prehensile lip to gather tall grass in bunches. When it is eating shorter grass, it is able to tuck the lip out of the way. The black rhinoceros in Africa is usually said to be exclusively a browsing animal, but it too is capable of eating smaller plants, such as clover, when the situation demands.

Horns and Fighting

The horns of rhinoceroses appeared late in their evolutionary history, though those of the white rhinoceros can reach an enormous size. The structure of the horn gives rise to a good deal of misunderstanding. It is not a horn in the conventional sense, having no bony central core. Instead, it consists of an aggregation of hollow keratin fibres, similar to hair, but lacking the outer cuticle. Each fibre is 0.01–0.02 in (0.3–0.5 mm) in diameter, and they are bonded together with a minimal amount of horn between the filaments. This makes the horn fray rather easily when it is worn, especially in the Indian and Javan rhinoceroses, whose horns are not sharply pointed like those of the African species.

Both African species sharpen their horns regularly, by stropping them on trees or on rocks. Wood sharpens the horn more effectively: rocks eventually wear it away to a blunt stub. Each horn is mounted on a roughened knob on the skull. If the horn is accidentally knocked off, it will grow again, especially in younger animals. The African and Sumatran species have two horns in tandem, while the Indian and the Javan have only one.

The use of the horn in fighting leads to some interesting conclusions about the development of ritualised conflict among heavily-armed animals. It has long been observed that gannets and colonially-nesting cormorants, for example, both fish-eating birds with long sharp bills, have elaborate threat behaviour which enables them to avoid actual violence while still settling disputes between individuals. The effect at the breeding ground is to space out the nests so that they are two bill-lengths apart: neither animal can reach the other to harm it, but both are able to maintain their social position.

The same is true of other animals which have weapons capable of inflicting severe wounds, so that both loser and winner of any fight might be physically damaged or even killed. White rhinoceroses have the most formidable horns of all and, as might be expected, they have the most ritualised confrontation behaviour. Two males at the boundary of their territories appear to stand nose to nose without any particular movement or aggression, before backing off to wipe their horns on the ground, after which they part. Male black rhinoceroses are not usually territorial, but they cross horns with females from time to time during courtship.

The difference between the white rhinoceros and the black in this respect has been traced to the difference in their diet, as it affects the amount of space which each species needs in order to find enough food. Grazing white rhinoceroses may build up quite large densities in their feeding areas, as many as five per 0.4 sq miles (1 sq km). This means that each occupies a relatively small territory, with the result that they meet often, and boundary disputes are common. Thus there is more need for some form of ritualised confrontation which stops short of actual conflict and does not threaten the combatants with injury. Their apparent inactivity during their 'staring matches' is in fact a subtle and precise contest in which each animal gauges the weight and strength of the other. It might be likened to arm-wrestling as a test of strength between human males. The horn-wiping which follows may be interpreted as a symbolic attack, in which only the preliminary lowering of the fearsome weapon remains. Sometimes the loser in a contest may make a similar gesture before retreating, as a form of redirected aggression.

Black rhinoceroses, which feed in woodland, do not meet each other so often. As

Figure 7: Horn-wrestling is a ritualised form of conflict, which permits a trial of strength without the risk of injury to either party

a browsing animal, the black rhinoceros needs a much larger range than the white to provide it with enough food: densities in the wild, even in well-stocked areas, rarely exceed one per 0.4 sq miles (1 sq km). The boundaries of territories can overlap, because they are not so frequently visited by the owner. Instead of fighting, or developing ritualised conflicts which simulate fighting, the black rhinoceros places more reliance on sign-posting his boundaries with urine.

The Indian rhinoceros has a different approach from that of both the black and the white: neighbouring males fight only rarely, but any intruder from outside is attacked with great ferocity. It feeds among the tall grasses which grow on drying flood plains beside rivers. The exact location of its feeding grounds is not predictable, as the water-level changes from season to season. Being a grazing animal, the Indian rhinoceros can build up densities on the feeding grounds as high as those of the white rhinoceros, but because it needs to be able to feed when and where the grass is growing best, it is more efficient for it not to be too dedicated to the idea of holding territory at all. Furthermore, the temptation to assert itself may be less because it seldom actually sees any rivals: in elephant grass 10 ft (3 m) tall, in which the visibility is almost nil, the Indian rhinoceros may be close to a potential adversary without the sight of it triggering an attack.

Although all five species of rhinoceros have some degree of ritualised conflict, there are records of tremendous fights between males, resulting in serious wounds to both combatants. African rhinoceroses fight by jabbing upwards with their horns, while the Asian species slash open-mouthed to attack with their incisors, or the canines in the case of the Javan rhinoceros.

In discussing the ritualisation of conflict, Kingdon has made the interesting point that animals which limit fighting by keeping out of each other's way, rather than by developing rituals which enable them to live closer together without actually coming to blows, may be missing an opportunity of exploiting their habitats more fully, since they are wasting space. This is a poor evolutionary strategy: there are therefore few examples of animals whose social behaviour is so explicitly violent and unrestrained. (Kingdon quotes the chevrotain — a primitive ungulate with large teeth, claws where the others have toenail-style hooves, and a fiercely combative nature.) In evolutionary terms, the black rhinoceros would

Figure 8: The gesture of wiping the horn may well symbolise the preliminary to an attack which is never carried out

benefit from developing a more strongly territorial social system, especially when food is in short supply. At Tsavo in East Africa, and in other overcrowded locations, more competition for the available food would have saved a large number of animals from starvation, even though it meant the death of a few less dominant individuals.

Chemical Markers

In male rhinoceroses the retracted penis is directed backwards; they can use it for spraying urine behind them on to bushes or on to the ground. Urine-spraying is an expression of dominance during and after conflicts, and a means of marking territorial boundaries at other times. The urine is produced in a fine spray, almost like an aerosol, scenting the air for some distance around, and lingering on the ground for days afterwards. Among white rhinoceroses, urine-spraying is the privilege of dominant males inside their own territories. Subordinate males, or senior bulls passing through the territories of others on their way to and from water, do not spray. The dominant male will recommence spraying only when he is once

Figure 9: Urine-spraying is the prerogative of dominant males, usually to mark the boundaries of a territory

more on his own ground. The details of urinary etiquette vary from species to species.

Dung is deposited in heaps at a number of selected spots within the territory, the biggest heaps being near the boundary. After defaecation, a dominant white rhinoceros bull kicks the dung with his hind feet, scattering it backwards. A long-established white rhinoceros dunghill or midden has grooves across it showing where the proprietor has repeatedly performed this ritual marking of his territory. The much less strongly territorial black rhinoceros rarely excludes others from his feeding range. Both male and female black rhinoceroses kick their dung after defaecation, and the males spray urine, but the function of their ritual is probably quite different. Some engaging experiments with bags of dung are described in the separate account of the black rhinoceros in Chapter 4.

Courtship and Breeding

The courtship and breeding of each species will also be described separately, so far as the details are available. However, there are some aspects which may be taken as part of the general rhinoceros way of life.

Wild rhinoceroses do not usually breed as fast as their physiology would allow. Single calves are the rule, though twins have very occasionally been seen, and although the interval between calves can in theory be as short as 22 months, most rhinoceroses breed every third or fourth year.

There is an intriguing difference between white and black rhinoceroses once their calves are born: the black rhinoceros calf follows its mother wherever she goes, trailing a few paces behind, while the white rhinoceros calf accompanies its mother just as closely, but almost always travels a few feet ahead of her. Rhinoceros calves remain with their mother after weaning, being dismissed from her company only when the next calf is born. After being turned out to face the world alone, the juveniles may join forces with one or more others of their own age, or attach themselves to a childless female. When they reach adulthood, they become solitary.

Rhinoceroses share some other features in common: they can all be categorised as uncompetitive animals, poorly adapted to resist the pressures which may develop when their habitat comes under pressure from over-population by another species, including (especially) humankind. They breed and grow slowly, making them unsuitable even for controlled exploitation as a resource. They are poor colonists, being conservative in their use of the available terrain: schemes to increase their numbers in selected areas must rely on the translocation of captured animals. However, they are valuable members of the ecosystems where they still survive in sufficient numbers to have any effect: for example, the tracks made through the bush by black rhinoceroses travelling to water are used by large numbers of other animals. Those made by Javan rhinoceroses many years ago are still used by human travellers; some of them have become the route of modern roads.

All rhinoceroses share the same major predator, and all are equally defenceless against and threatened by its attentions. Until the human species stops killing them for medicines and dagger handles, the fate of the world's rhinoceroses is in the balance. The most likely outcome of the present rate of predation by humans is extinction for all but the white rhinoceros before the end of this century. Paradoxically, perhaps, the greatest hope for the two African species may be that a few of them every year should become trophies on the wall of the den of a number of very wealthy hunters: I shall explore this paradox further towards the end of the book.

4
The Black Rhinoceros

▼▼

THE BLACK RHINOCEROS
Scientific name: *Diceros bicornis*
Common names: Black rhinoceros, Prehensile-lipped rhinoceros,
Browse rhinoceros

Range and numbers (1984 figures)

Tanzania	3,130
Zimbabwe	1,680
Zambia	1,650
South Africa	640
Kenya	550
Namibia	400
Central African Republic	170
Mozambique	130
Cameroon	110
Sudan	100
Somalia	90
Angola	90
Malawi	20
Rwanda	15
Botswana	10
Ethiopia	10
Chad	5
Total in 17 countries	8,800

Source: Western and Vigne (1985), Oryx 19,
215–20.

Length of head and body	10 ft–12 ft 6 in	(3.0–3.8 m)
Height at shoulder	4 ft 6 in–6 ft	(1.4–1.8 m)
Weight	2,195–3,000 lb	(996–1,362 kg)
Length of front horn	1 ft 8 in–4 ft 4 in	(50–135 cm)

Distribution and Status

The black rhinoceros is no more black than the white rhinoceros is white. When it was described, by Linnaeus in 1758, it was called the two-horned rhinoceros, the only other known species being the Indian one-horned. It seems to have absorbed its misleading common name by contrast with the misnamed white rhinoceros when that species was discovered. The name 'white' is a corruption of the Afrikaans *weit*, which describes the *wide* mouth of the species. Kingdon used the names 'browse rhinoceros' and 'grass rhinoceros' for black and white respectively: these names are far more descriptive than 'black' and 'white', and easier on the tongue than such heavy-handed titles as 'prehensile-lipped' and 'square-lipped' for the

▲▲

Plate 2: The snows of Kilimanjaro look down across plains which are now virtually denuded of black rhinoceroses. This photograph was taken in the mid-seventies when the species was fairly common.

Plate 3: Although they occasionally compete for water, giraffes and rhinoceroses can ignore each other ecologically because they exploit different niches.

two species. Nevertheless, in this account, I shall stick to the familiar 'black' and 'white', misleading though they are as names. In due course Kingdon's names will probably be used, as they become better known.

Even today, there is some uncertainty about whether the two species are different enough to be separated into two distinct genera, but at the end of the nineteenth century there was a brisk argument among zoologists about the taxonomy of the black rhinoceros itself, some claiming that there were two species in Africa, the black rhinoceros proper, *Rhinoceros bicornis*, and the 'blue', *R. keitloa*. The difference between them was supposed to be in the relative length of their horns. In a typically strongly argued paper, which he read to the Zoological Society of London in 1881, Selous demonstrated (with the aid of a collection of horns some of which came from animals that he had shot himself) that they are both the same species. A wider knowledge of the species has since shown that individuals vary in size, and in the size of their horns, partly at least in response to local conditions, tending to be smaller in drier habitats. Nowadays they are both included in the single species *Diceros bicornis*.

The black rhinoceros is separated from the white by its ecological requirements, even when the two species inhabit the same general area. As a browser, it can colonise areas of rugged hilly terrain where grass is scarce, up to heights of 9,000 ft (2,700 m). It avoids both the open grassland used by the white rhinoceros, and

Figure 10: The black rhinoceros has a prehensile upper lip, typical of a browsing animal. However, it can also feed on fruits, and plants such as clover

very dense cover, preferring the edges of small wooded areas. Thus, originally, it had a very wide range, which covered the southern third of Africa, and stretched northwards between the east side of the Rift Valley and the east coast. North of there, the species inhabited a broad band of open woodlands stretching from the Horn of Africa to the west coast south of the Sahara.

Towards the end of his first visit to South Africa, Selous, although himself a hunter, became alarmed by the impact of hunting, and the sharp decline which he had witnessed in both species of rhinoceros. He remarked as early as 1881 that the black rhinoceros had been 'almost exterminated in the westerly portions of the country', though it was still fairly numerous in the south-east. By the turn of the century, its range had contracted still further. It was rare or extinct in the north-western and north-eastern extremes of its range, and disappearing fast in the south, as the result of very heavy shooting pressure from the white settlers there. By then, the only sizeable populations were to be found in East Africa: the numbers dwindled further north in the Sudan and Somalia. Today, as described below, the range of the black rhinoceros is contracting so fast that it would be better recorded in a daily newspaper rather than a book, which takes time to get into print. The only countries in which it is anything like secure, in spite of its earlier near-extinction in those regions, are South Africa, Namibia and Zimbabwe; though

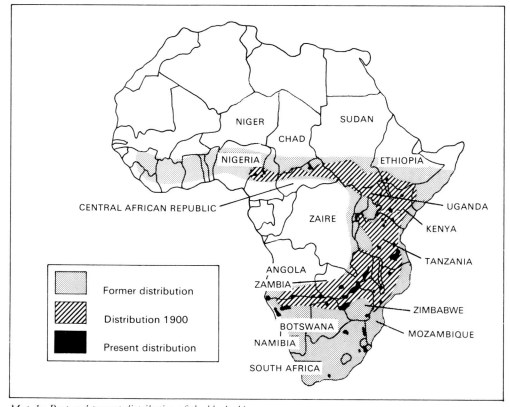

Map 1: Past and present distribution of the black rhinoceros

even in Zimbabwe it is under heavy attack from organised poachers.

There was a time when the range of the black rhinoceros was determined by the climatic conditions: it inhabited forests and woodland everywhere unless they were too dry, as in parts of East Africa, or too hot and humid, like the lowland forests to the west of the Rift Valley. Now, its range is determined by the reach of the financial resources of countries to whom the horn is valuable as the material for dagger handles.

Diet

The black rhinoceros is usually described as a browsing animal, a method of feeding for which it is conspicuously well-adapted. It feeds on leaves and twigs from a wide variety of shrubs in the acacia woodland community, often using its horn to pull down and even break branches until their ends come within reach of its prehensile upper lip. In open grassland, it pulls up seedlings of colonising trees, thus improving the pasture for itself and other grazing animals. However, it has a wider diet than this when circumstances permit: it will pick up fallen fruits from the ground as well as taking those which it can reach from trees, and it is able to feed on grass which is long enough to be twisted together into bundles. Green clover and other herbs are acceptable if they are all that is available.

Black rhinoceroses, in the Ngorongoro Crater in Tanzania, have been known to pick up and eat wildebeeste dung, during periods when browse is in short supply, and the grass has been cropped too closely by other species for the rhinoceroses to eat. Such behaviour might have satisfied a need for minerals and trace elements; but equally there might have been a good deal of sustenance still remaining in the droppings.

During the rainy season, the black rhinoceros ranges freely, feeding over a wide area. When the dry weather comes, it stays within 3 miles (5 km) of permanent water. It needs to drink once a day, or even more often if possible, following regular routes between its feeding and watering places. In especially arid conditions, black rhinoceroses can dig for water, using their front feet to throw the sand out behind them until they have made a hole which might be as much as 20 in (50 cm) deep.

The tracks which black rhinoceroses use as they travel through the bush are followed by many other species, either to go to and from the same watering hole, or just as convenient passages. There is often a groove in the ground about 20 in (50 cm) wide, and as much as 14 in (30 cm) deep, beneath a tunnel through the bushes 6 ft (180 cm) high. The advantage to the other animals is twofold: following an already cleared track saves them effort, but it also enables them to move quietly and less conspicuously.

Unlike the other animals of the bush, the black rhinoceros seems to take a particular delight in crashing through cover. Having no regular predators as an adult, it has no need to move stealthily; and there is a suggestion that by brushing against the vegetation it leaves a scented trail consisting of flakes of mud and pieces of dead skin which, together with sprayed urine and traces of dung, communicate its presence, and possibly also its identity, to the next rhinoceros to come along.

Daily Routine

The daily routine of the black rhinoceros is very similar to that which the white rhinoceros follows in hot weather. It feeds morning and evening, and sleeps in shade or in a wallow during the heat of the day. The species has become largely nocturnal in most parts of its range, probably as the result of natural selection, which has eliminated the more diurnal individuals which were the most likely to be shot. Accounts by early hunters mention meeting black rhinoceroses regularly by day during the first years of the Europeans' exploration of the lands north of the Cape; but in later years, before the rhinoceroses were so nearly wiped out, they were more likely to hear them moving around or drinking during the night.

As early as 1873, Selous was moved by the sight of a group of elephants drinking in daylight. He writes in his account of that year: '. . . what a glorious sight it must have been to see these gigantic animals walking in the open with their slow majestic step' — and he was one of the first hunters to venture into that part of Africa. When their persecution comes to an end, black rhinoceroses will no doubt resume a more diurnal way of life, as elephants have done in parks where they are protected, and as black rhinoceroses themselves have in parks such as Hwange in Zimbabwe.

Because rhinoceroses cannot sweat, they need regular access to water to keep cool. Wallowing plays an important part in the life of the black rhinoceros, as it does in other species. As well as helping to lower the body temperature, it probably gives some protection against flies, not only during the process but afterwards, when a coating of dried mud must offer some barrier to biting insects. Whether it 'conditions' the skin, as most people say, is open to conjecture: rolling between wallowing sessions may be more important in this respect.

Like the white rhinoceros, the black rolls regularly in dust or ash, probably as a form of grooming. 'Rhino sores', areas of cracked and often inflamed skin, occur most commonly in the hollow behind the elbows of the front legs, the one area which is not scrubbed by a roll on a patch of sandy or gritty ground. However, the skin between the thickened shield plates is remarkably thin and flexible, and might well benefit from regular damping.

Social Behaviour and Status

Black rhinoceroses have a different social organisation from that of the white rhinoceros. The males are solitary, but they do not hold territories in the strict sense of the word. Each has a preferred feeding area, whose boundaries usually overlap with those of its neighbours, but the breeding territory is not as clearly defined as that of the white rhinoceros. Males which make regular use of the same waterhole live in what have been called 'clans', loose communities centred around the waterhole. Each clan covers an area about 3 miles (5 km) in radius, that being the maximum distance which each rhinoceros is prepared to walk each day to reach permanent water. Within the clan, males seem to know each other, and to tolerate the presence in passing of one of their own. A male outsider wandering into the clan area will be challenged if he meets one of the resident males; intruding females are challenged less strongly.

The home range of female black rhinoceroses varies in size depending on the availability of food: in the thickest bush which is suitable for the species it might be as little as 1.2 sq miles (3 sq km), but in more arid country, with sparse cover, as much as 34.7 sq miles (90 sq km) may be occupied by a female and her calf.

Except where they gather in wallows, black rhinoceroses do not form large groups: five is the largest party usually seen together, though groups of as many as 13 have been recorded, probably a temporary assembly as two or more groups met. Females travel with their last calf close at heel, occasionally accompanied by the previous calf if it was a female. Family groups of this kind need a larger feeding range than single animals, and probably for this reason females with young are notably more aggressive towards other rhinoceroses.

A young animal which has been displaced by the birth of its mother's next offspring is usually driven away, but instead of wandering off alone through the bush, it pairs up with another, of either sex, usually near its own age. The two may then wander long distances from their birthplace before settling down to the normally sedentary life of their species.

Encounters between male black rhinoceroses are very rarely aggressive, unless a stranger wanders into a clan area. If this happens, the animal which is on its home ground is usually successful in driving the intruder away. Snorting and pawing the ground are the prelude to a series of short charges, which usually stop about 20 ft (6 m) short of impact. Sometimes the intruder will charge as well, but the two animals seldom make contact: instead they adopt stiff-legged poses, tails in the air, until the tension between them gradually relaxes, and one moves calmly away.

However, during a time of ecological stress in East Tsavo, before the drought of 1960–1, all the rhinoceroses were found to be wounded, and some were killed in fights. This was evidently abnormal behaviour, produced by conditions of extreme hardship.

There is a dominance hierarchy among neighbouring bulls, similar to the pecking order among ground-feeding birds. There is more than one level of subservience, but postures and symbolic charges replace fighting in maintaining each bull's position in society. Sometimes a dominant intruder may displace one of the members of the resident clan. If this happens, the defeated animal moves off and challenges the occupant of the next range, until the social system has settled down once more.

Breeding

Most fights between adult rhinoceroses involve animals of opposite sex. The Kenyan naturalist, C. A. W. Guggisberg, made a study of the courtship and mating behaviour of the black rhinoceros, and found that cows often attack bulls which are making advances towards them. However, he also gives a dramatic account of a violent conflict, between a cow and a bull known as 'Split ear', in which the bull was the aggressor.

The battle began when the bull, which was to be seen regularly with the same cow, started showing signs of excitement — snorting, and opening his mouth and curling his lip in what Guggisberg calls a 'sexual yawn'. The first attack was very short, ending with the two animals standing nose to nose, after which the bull backed off, rubbed his nose on the ground, scraped with his hind legs; defaecated, and scraped again.

After a time he began circling the cow, snorting continuously and twisting his tail over his rump. During most of this display the female stood as motionless as a statue. When she once turned towards 'Split ear' in an aggressive manner, he trampled with all four feet on the spot he stood on, looking for all the world as if he were dancing. A few moments later he launched another attack. But the cow drove him back, opening her mouth wide and uttering the same snarling sound I had once heard in the Lake Manyara National Park, a sound that might be rendered as *chrachrachrachrachra*, the 'ch' to be pronounced as in 'Loch'. 'Split ear' again rubbed his nose in the grass and shredded the surrounding bushes with his horn. This game went on for some time, accompanied by a lot of snorting and snarling.

The fight became more and more violent, with both contestants playing an equal part, attacking the other with shoulders and horns. The bull actually lifted the cow with his head more than once, so that only her back legs were on the ground. The contest lasted for four or five minutes before the cow ran away, the bull charging after her. Soon, they were fighting again, but finally the cow seemed to surrender.

She stood motionless, while 'Split ear' walked around, rubbing his nose on the ground, ploughing up the grass and tossing whole loads of branches into the air. He sprayed a bush, scraped several times, and worked himself into such a state that he finally advanced once more upon the cow. This time she did not snarl her defiance, but retreated before him, walking backwards. 'Split ear' quietened down almost at once, and when we left the battlefield, with dusk descending on the plains, he was ambling about rather aimlessly.

Courtship does not always involve fighting, though most females respond violently to the male's first approaches. The male's usual preliminary to an attempt to mount is to lay his head across the female's back. This is preceded by a courtship display which consists of brushing the ground with his horn, charging at bushes, and darting back and forward on stiff legs, frequently spraying urine. This war-dance seems to have the effect of rousing the male to the point at which he dares to make the final advance: but it evidently affects the female as well, giving rise to what may often be a violent response.

However, the display seems to have little effect on nearby males, which rarely fight over oestrus females. In a recognisable group of rhinoceroses, it was found that one cow was courted, if not actually mounted, by three different bulls in eleven days. The significant observation during this period was that the male who first mounted her showed no interest or concern while she was being courted by the others, even though he was close at hand. There seems to be no sexual jealousy among black rhinoceros males; but that may be because members of a clan know each other well, and have often tested their relative strengths. They therefore have no need to fight repeatedly to remember which must give way to which in the social hierarchy.

Evidently the female can play a more active role in courtship: there is an account of a courting pair of rhinoceroses which were disturbed by suddenly becoming

Figure 11: Black rhinoceroses mate for 20 to 35 minutes at a time, several times a day

aware that they were being watched by some people in a car. The male, on getting wind of the car, turned and trotted off into the bush; but the female, apparently unaware that he had gone, performed a series of alluring gestures to the car, tossing grass with her mouth, and strutting stiff-legged towards it. When she, too, smelled the car, her behaviour changed abruptly: she charged, hitting it with a loud crash, before leaving the scene with angry snorts.

Black rhinoceroses have often been seen mating in zoos, though only rarely in the wild. In Frankfurt Zoo, copulation lasted from 20 to 35 minutes, and took place several times a day, figures which agree with occasional sightings in the wild. Wild pairs have been seen to move around together for as long as four months, but more often the male wanders away after a few days.

There is a famous account of the 'altruistic' behaviour of three female rhinoceroses towards a fourth, seen in Nairobi National Park in 1958. Three of them were walking close together, the middle one supported by the other two, while the fourth walked close behind. The middle female was in labour, and one of the others kept rubbing her flank with the side of her head and her horn. Three days later, a newly-born calf was found close by.

No one has ever seen a wild rhinoceros giving birth, and the chances are that very few other rhinoceroses have seen it either. The mother-to-be hides when her calf is due, retiring into thick cover, usually alone: the Nairobi National Park incident is the only report of midwifery among rhinoceroses. Most descriptions date back to the first successful captive birth, in Brookfield Zoo, Chicago, in 1941. Since then, black rhinoceroses have bred in captivity regularly, and a good deal of information has been gathered which, though interesting, need not necessarily represent what happens in the wild.

Gestation is between 446 and 548 days, depending on the zoo which provides the information: the average seems to be 460 days, or about 15 months. Presumably the uncertainty arises from the fact that no zoo keeper has ever been sure when his female charges have been impregnated. Copulation takes place at regular intervals of three and a half weeks throughout pregnancy, suggesting that the oestrus cycle is uninterrupted.

Mating and birth occur throughout the year. The mother remains secluded for a couple of weeks, defending her newborn baby against all comers. Bulls in zoos have been known to attack small calves: there is nothing to say that this is typical behaviour for the species, but if it were, it would explain the mother's reclusive behaviour. She avoids wallowing while she is suckling a small calf, probably for hygienic reasons. She has two teats, between her hind legs, and she normally suckles the calf standing up.

The previous calf is driven away by its mother when she produces her next: at this time it might be anything between two and five years old, but still not fully grown. The newborn calf weighs between 55–88 lb (25–40 kg), about four per cent of its mother's weight: this is typical of all species of rhinoceros. Although it can stand and walk within ten minutes of being born, the calf is plainly very vulnerable to accidental (or deliberate) trampling. The young calf stays very close to its mother at all times, following her movements closely: if danger threatens, the female swings sideways to interpose her body between her calf and the approaching predator. Later in the calf's life, this behaviour causes the radial formation, horns outwards, which is the typical response of a group of black rhinoceroses at bay: each is trying to protect the one next to it by standing broadside on.

Black rhinoceroses are usually fully grown at about seven years of age, though one in London Zoo was still growing at nine years old. They reach sexual maturity at about six or seven. A male's chance of breeding depends on his position in the social hierarchy, but a female can breed before she is fully grown. In the wild, a

Figure 12: The black rhinoceros calf follows its mother, perhaps as an adaptation to travelling through thick cover: she is better able to clear the way

female breeds only every two to five years, because of the time required to rear the calf; in a wild population, a quarter of the females breed each year. Their life expectancy is not accurately known, but in zoos black rhinoceroses can live for 40 years. Guggisberg estimated that two females which he knew at Amboseli, who were known to staff and visitors as Gladys and Gertie, were between 20 and 30 years old when he first met them in 1954, and in 1966 they were both alive and well. His estimate of their likely longevity was between 50 and 60 years.

Unfortunately, they did not live for so long. They were speared to death by a group of Masai, not much more than a year after Guggisberg last saw them. Although their horns were taken and undoubtedly sold for profit, the main motivation for the killing, so the naturalist/cameraman Alan Root tells me, was defiance or bravado on the part of the warriors who were responsible. This common and unfortunate response by rural Africans to the establishment of game reserves is discussed further in Chapter 11.

Signs and Signals

The sounds made by black rhinoceroses are not as varied as those of the white, but apart from puffing and snorting they have a few vocalisations whose function may be guessed at. Calves and their mothers communicate with a variety of squeals. A calf which had lost sight of its mother repeated a faint sound which has been described as 'mfee', a pathetic bleat from an animal which was three-quarters grown, and weighed at least 1,650 lb (750 kg). In moments of panic, a calf can produce a loud and penetrating squeal: males will come to investigate this sound from as much as half a mile (a kilometre) or so away. Fighting adults grunt and scream at each other; and adults approaching waterholes where others are already wallowing make a puffing or gasping sound which may serve to avoid conflicts by giving the group an early warning of their approach.

The most frequent signals used by the black rhinoceros are based on scent. Urine-spraying is very common along their trails to and from water, especially by dominant males within their feeding territory. Bushes, clumps of grass, tree stumps and conspicuous stones are all marked regularly, often during the male's morning tour of his borders. Females spray when they are in oestrus, no doubt to announce their condition to nearby bulls, but their spraying is undirected, and in the form of a jet of liquid rather than the forceful aerosol puff produced by males. Similarly, when they are defending their young from the attentions of other adults, females produce scent-signals which are delivered at random into the air.

The use of dung as a means of signalling is similar in black and white rhinoceroses. Black rhinoceroses use communal dung-heaps beside their regular tracks through the bush; in places where both black and white share the same area, these communal heaps may be used by both species. Scraping with the hind legs is a common piece of behaviour after defaecation; its function is not to conceal the droppings, but rather to make them more conspicuous. Furthermore, by picking up the scent of his droppings on his hind feet, a male rhinoceros might be able to leave his individual imprint on a considerable length of trail, in much the same way as the urine-sprays, for the benefit of later passers-by.

There have been some experiments to find the function of dung-scented trails.

▼▼

Biologists towed bags of the dung of known individuals through the bush for distances of up to half a mile (a kilometre), observing the effect on other rhinoceroses in the area. They found that the animals would follow the scent left by the bags much more intently and for longer distances if the dung was from a member of their own clan, or another individual with which they had regular contact. Dung from rhinoceroses which lived further away, outside their immediate social circle, aroused much less interest. This suggests that the identity of an individual animal is apparent to another from the scent of his droppings, and no doubt also from his urine. Scenting the area in both ways must provide to passers-by a constantly updated record of the population present, including the sexual condition of the females.

Parasites and Predators

Black rhinoceroses are particularly vulnerable to 'rhino sores', which are usually just behind and below the shoulder, in the area which they find most difficult to scratch while rolling. The sores are inflamed, often septic, patches of skin, as much as 8 in (20 cm) in diameter, which are infested with a small filariform worm called *Stephanofilaria dinniki*. The five other species of this genus of worm are all parasites of cattle: the intermediate host is a biting fly which breeds in dung. In visiting the communal dung-heaps along their trails, the rhinoceroses pass the infection around the population: almost every individual has sores caused by this worm.

Over 20 species of ticks have been found feeding on black rhinoceroses, some of them specific to the rhinoceros, and others impartial parasites on elephants as well. The ticks provide a regular food-supply for oxpeckers, birds related to starlings. Every rhinoceros carries two or three of these grey-brown birds, with their bright orange beaks, pecking industriously at the ticks on its skin. The birds not only remove the parasites; they also cause the rhinoceros some discomfort, by sticking their sharp beaks into ears and nostrils, and pecking at any open wounds or sores. However, they perform a service of another kind by acting as an alarm system. Although they have become accustomed to cars in game parks, in the same way as the rhinoceroses themselves, in open hunting areas the oxpeckers fly up with loud screeching calls when humans approach.

There is a reported sighting from Natal of a female black rhinoceros which was being cleaned of ticks by turtles as she lay in a wallow; in one case, six turtles were to be seen climbing on to the rhinoceros' body to pull the ticks out in their mouths.

Among its internal parasites, the black rhinoceros numbers bot-flies, whose larvae live in its stomach, and several species of tapeworm.

The black rhinoceros has few predators. Lions have been known to kill adults, and to take a calf if they can separate it from its mother; but her defensive behaviour is such that this is a rare event. A more serious predator is the spotted hyaena, which takes calves so successfully that it seriously restricts population growth. In areas where the breeding of black rhinoceroses is a primary aim of park managers, it is usually necessary to control or eliminate the spotted hyaena.

There is a collection of stories about battles between black rhinoceroses and other species of animal, especially elephants, which have been supposed since classical times to be their sworn enemies. Some of these stories should be taken with

▲▲

a pinch of salt, but other accounts come from reliable eye-witnesses. Guggisberg, for example, was shown a rhinoceros which had been drowned by a hippopotamus; the hippo had evidently dragged the rhinoceros into the water by one leg, and killed it with its tusks. Selous published a series of photographs showing a fully grown female rhinoceros being dragged into a pool by a crocodile. There are several reliable accounts of elephants killing rhinoceroses, and folk wisdom has it that, although bull elephants tolerate them, female elephants simply cannot stand their presence.

The supposed ferocity of the black rhinoceros is another fruitful source of travellers' tales. Alan Root has told me of several serious attacks recently in game parks in Kenya and Tanzania, and the literature is full of hunters' stories of fatal attacks and narrow escapes. On the other hand, there are stories which stress the element of bluff in the charge of a rhinoceros. The chief factor which makes the black rhinoceros more dangerous than the white is its habitat: in thick bush it is more likely to be taken by surprise than the white rhinoceros in open grassland. It can charge very nimbly at up to 30 miles (50 km) per hour, and will attack with its horn any unidentified object. People on foot in the bush are extremely vulnerable, but cars have also been severely damaged by startled animals. Some of the earlier accounts mention that the attacking animal had been wounded by an inefficient hunter, but recent reports are from protected areas where there is no hunting, and poaching is rare. It is tempting to conclude that the apparent change in the reaction of the black rhinoceros to the scent of humans, from its timid curiosity in the reports by Selous to the ferocity which is so often reported nowadays, is the result of its maltreatment by our species. It may indeed be true that natural selection favours individuals which can keep humans at a distance. Whatever the truth, the conflicting evidence suggests that prudence is the most sensible course. Wandering about in trackless bush, or, worse, in bush with rhinoceros tracks, is to invite attack.

The greatest enemy of the black rhinoceros is mankind. Because its favoured habitat is fertile and well-watered, it has come into conflict with humans since long before the arrival of Europeans in Africa. Its uncertain behaviour must have made it an alarming neighbour to cattle-herders, and its feeding habits make it a threat to crops such as cotton. As the human population grows — and that of Kenya is growing fastest in all Africa — the demand for land for settlement is increasing, and with it the call for the control or elimination of rhinoceroses. However, the level of poaching is such that the problem is solving itself, from the point of view of those who would rather not share their land with rhinoceroses: there will soon be none left outside the parks and reserves, if indeed they can be protected there.

5
The White Rhinoceros

▼▼▼

THE WHITE RHINOCEROS
Scientific name: *Ceratotherium simum*
Common names: White rhinoceros, Square-lipped rhinoceros,
Grass rhinoceros

Range and numbers

Southern race: 1984 figures

South Africa	3,330
Botswana	200
Zimbabwe	200
Namibia	70
Swaziland	60
Kenya	30
Mozambique	20
Zambia	10

Northern race: 1986 figures

Zaire	17
Total in 9 countries	3,937

Source: Oryx 19, 4; WWF Yearbook 1985/86

Length of head and body (males larger)	12–14 ft	(3.6–4.2 m)
Height at shoulder	5–6 ft	(1.5–1.85 m)
Weight	5,070–7,936 lb	(2,300–3,600 kg)
Length of front horn (northern race)	37–40 in	(95–101 cm)
(southern race)	37–79 in	(95–200 cm)

Distribution and Status

The common name of the white rhinoceros has nothing to do with its colour, but derives instead from the Afrikaans word describing its mouth: *weit*, meaning 'wide'. It is adapted to graze short grass, with a mouth like the business end of a lawnmower, and it would seem to be the ideal large herbivore for huge areas of African grasslands.

There is good evidence that the distribution of the white rhinoceros was once much wider than it is now. Cave paintings have been found in the northern and central Sahara, in Tanzania, and in the Kalahari which are clearly intended as portraits of this species. Even before Europeans began to explore southern and central Africa, it had disappeared from some of those areas, perhaps from over-hunting, or possibly from changes in the vegetation during droughts. It needs large quantities of food and it depends on permanent water: it is possible that having

▲▲▲

died out in certain areas during particularly severe droughts it was unable to recolonise them in the face of competition from more efficient animals which could move more freely to exploit such food and water as was available. Its territorial behaviour and rather slow rate of breeding make it a poor colonist, very slow to expand its range at the best of times.

The species was described in South Africa in 1817, but it was not discovered in Uganda until 1907. It is generally considered as being one species with two races, geographically separated but not markedly different in appearance or way of life.

Selous noted the rapid decline in the numbers of the white rhinoceros between the years 1872 and 1877 in southern Africa. During his expedition in the region of the Upper Chobe River in 1879, where he found no trace of white rhinoceroses, all the Bushmen whom he met said that they were 'finished'. He found a few later between the Umniati and Hanyane Rivers, in what was then called North-eastern Mashuna Land, now western Zimbabwe. Although the names of many of the rivers have changed since the time of Selous, the Umniati is still as he knew it, and from the rest of his description the remnant animals were not far from what is now Hwange National Park.

The present distribution of the species is in two parts: the northern race, which is extinct except in Zaire, where 17 individuals survive in Garamba National Park, and the southern race south of the Zambesi. In 1984 the northern race survived in Sudan (10), Uganda and the Central African Republic (1 each). There was a

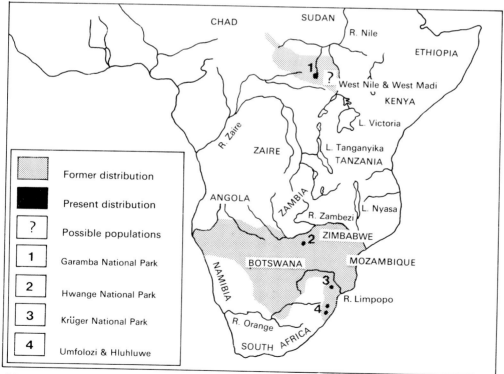

Map 2: Past and present distribution of the white rhinoceros

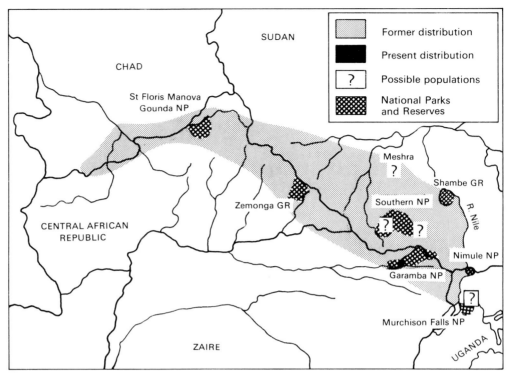

Map 3: Past and present distribution of the northern white rhinoceros

refuge at Waka Swamp, on the flood plain of the Nile, where the last survivors in the area were protected, but between 1984 and 1986 they were wiped out by poachers. Their decline in the north is relatively recent: the early white hunters avoided the area because it was so heavily infested with malarial mosquitoes, and the local people had no use for the animal until a demand grew for horns for medical and, much more recently, ornamental uses. The peak of rhinoceros poaching for this market came in the early 1950s, and by the early 1960s numbers had fallen so low that poaching had almost come to a stop for lack of animals to hunt. There was another burst of poaching during the 1980s in Sudan and Zaire, which left only the Garamba animals alive.

In 1980, the populations of the northern race were as follows: Central African Republic 20 (now 0); Sudan 400 (now 0); Uganda 1 (now 0); and Zaire 400. The world population of the northern race has fallen from 821 to 17 in just six years.

The story of the southern race is completely different. Selous was right in his gloomy prediction of its imminent disappearance, but the danger was spotted by other people as well, and the decline was halted in time. The remnant population which survived in Zululand was used as the nucleus from which a thriving new population has been built up in Natal. From a low point in the 1920s, the southern race of the white rhinoceros has grown to a stable and expanding population: in the same period, 1980 to 1984, during which the northern race almost disappeared, the southern race grew from 3,020 to 3,920, an increase of nearly 30 per cent: 830 of

Plate 4: Moving rhinoceroses requires detailed planning and care in the use of tranquillizing drugs. An animal left for too long on the ground may suffer irreparable damage to the nerves of its legs.

Plate 5: 'Rhino sores' are infected areas of skin, infested with a worm which is transmitted by biting flies which breed in the rhinoceroses' communal dung-heaps.

Plate 6 : Black rhino in the Amboseli National Park, Kenya. Both the size of the animal and the length of its horns are directly related to the aridity of its environment.

these animals were born in South Africa. The story of 'Operation Rhino' is given in full at the end of this chapter.

Daily Routine

In cool weather, white rhinoceroses feed and rest alternately, for a few hours at a time, day and night. With the approach of the hot dry weather, the rest period near the middle of the day becomes more of a fixed point, until at the height of the dry season the animals are feeding in the cool of morning and evening, and dozing through the rest of the day. They feed more during the night at this time of year, to make up for lost time during the heat of the day.

Much of their resting time is spent wallowing to keep cool. Rhinoceroses need water for drinking and wallowing at least every two to four days, and if their feeding areas are dry, they will walk as far as 6 miles (10 km) from their home range to find it, following regular paths through the bush. The hollows where water gathers on a hardpan surface are used by other wallowing species, such as buffalo and warthogs: between them, the animals maintain a short grass turf around waterholes which provides regular food for the grazing animals. It has the secondary advantage of reducing the cover which can be used by approaching predators.

At certain times of the year, when the flies are particularly troublesome, the rhinoceroses may elect to keep away from the shady, damp places which would otherwise attract them, in favour of more exposed places where a breeze keeps the insects at bay. When there is no water for wallowing or grooming purposes, they will roll in dust, presumably to keep their skin clear of ticks and other parasites. All white rhinoceroses use rubbing posts regularly, partly to control skin parasites, but

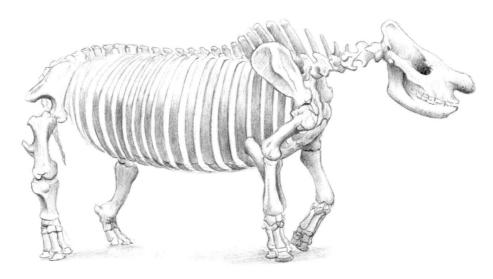

Figure 13: Pillar-like legs with massive muscle attachments give the white rhinoceros its strength and remarkable agility

in the case of dominant males probably also as a means of marking territory by leaving flakes of skin bearing their individual odour.

While they are on the move, whether walking or trotting, white rhinoceroses keep their heads down in the same position as when they are grazing. They look up only when they are alarmed, producing the familiar hump-backed outline where the huge neck and back muscles contract to lift the heavy head. They can gallop at as much as 25 miles (40 km) per hour for short periods, and they are surprisingly agile: one repeatedly climbed a gate 6 ft (2 m) high to escape from temporary captivity.

Social Behaviour and Status

The daily life of a white rhinoceros is regulated by its sex and its position within the social structure of the area. Dominant or *alpha* males hold feeding territories from which they exclude all other adult males. Their concern is not purely to make sure that they have enough food for themselves: the feeding territories will later become their breeding territories, within which they will defend a mate. White rhinoceroses rarely fight, but they often indulge in trials of strength, wrestling with their horns, or charging each other with their shoulders, to settle disputes, and to confirm their social position.

The size of a feeding territory depends on the quality of the food which can be found in it, and on the density of the animals, especially if they are enclosed in a park or in some other restricted area. Typically, where the population of white rhinoceroses is at full density, a male's feeding territory is about $\frac{3}{4}$ sq mile (2 sq km).Subsidiary males may feed within these territories, provided that they respond to challenges from the resident males by making the correct submissive gestures and sounds. After a dispute, the defeated male stops spraying urine or scattering dung, and utters a series of small high-pitched growls. He may then stay in the defended area to feed, if he keeps out of the proprietor's way. Males remain subsidiary in society from the time when they mature sexually, at about seven years of age, until they can displace an existing bull, inheriting his territory and his females, about three years later.

Young rhinoceroses, referred to as subadults, have a privileged position in society, presumably because they are not seen as a direct threat to the resident male's security. They can often encroach on to an alpha male's territory without incurring a full challenge: and if they are challenged, they are able to run away, unlike adult subsidiaries, which are compelled by several factors to stand their ground. The subadult's greatest advantage is superior mobility: quite simply, he can run faster than an adult bull. He can thus turn tail and take off without risking an attack from behind.

The fully adult but socially inferior subsidiary is too slow on his feet to run: but he must stand his ground for another reason as well. In fully occupied terrain, there is nowhere for him to go. Next door there is another defended territory in which his plight will be exactly the same. He therefore has no option but to stay where he is, look and sound submissive, and wait for the dominant male to tire of staring him down. It was estimated that 30 per cent of adult males in a crowded park in Zululand lived in this way, as tolerated subsidiaries in other males' territories.

Figure 14: The broad lips of a white rhinoceros enable it to graze short turf. Its wide mouth gave the species its Afrikaans, and later its English, name

The position of the females is different. They too have feeding ranges which are quite clearly defined, but much larger than those of the males. They may move about within a range of about 4 sq miles (10 sq km), passing through male territories without being challenged. The boundaries of these female ranges overlap freely, and mothers with calves are tolerant of each other's presence.

When a female gives birth to a new calf, she chases the previous calf away. By this time, it is two years old, fully weaned, and able to join the subadult society which is typical of white rhinoceroses.

The young rhinoceros has a certain number of options open to it at this age. Some find a companion, usually of the same sex as well as age, but others attach themselves to a childless female, which seems to function as an 'aunt', or quasi-foster mother. Some such females acquire more than one young companion, sometimes as many as five. In good feeding areas, or often at wallows, these gatherings form a focus for all passing subadults, as if they were the equivalent of a youth club, where playful wrestling and greeting behaviour are the order of the day. Sights such as this have led some authors to conclude that white rhinoceroses are gregarious animals; for short periods they are, but more typically they move in small groups of females and young of various ages, wending their way between the solitary males.

Breeding

Females are sexually mature at about seven years of age. When they come into oestrus they begin to spray urine while passing through male-held territories, advertising their condition and inviting courtship from the dominant males. A female with a calf comes into oestrus about six or eight months after giving birth. Mating takes place all the year round, with peaks at times when there is a flush of good green grass. In South Africa, this is between October and December: further north, the peak occurs between February and June.

Courtship is a slow and cautious ritual, taking between five and twenty days to complete. The male behaves cautiously for two reasons: he is threatened not only by the female, but also by her calf, which at over six months old is distinctly possessive: it is still nursing from its mother, and will continue to do so for another six months or more. The male corrals the female by repeatedly chasing her back from his boundary with loud wailing calls.

Males have been reported to attack young calves, and the calf is in danger of being killed by the furious bull during courtship. The mother protects her calf from the time when it is first born, by standing over it, and as it grows bigger, from close beside it. When an oestrus cow is in a group in the territory of an alpha male, the action can become confused, as each cow seeks to protect the young rhinoceros beside her: the end result is often to leave the animals standing in a ring, horns outwards, a position often reported by early hunters as evidence of the loyalty of white rhinoceroses to one another.

Eventually the bull overcomes the aggression of the female sufficiently to complete his courtship, by laying his head across her back, and eventually mounting her. Copulation takes as long as half an hour, after which the female moves out of the bull's territory, taking her calf with her.

The gestation period of the white rhinoceros is 16 months. By the time the mother is ready to give birth to her new calf, her previous offspring is two years old, and ready to move into the next phase of its social life. Its mother chases it off just

Figure 15. The white rhinoceros calf always walks ahead of its mother as they travel round their territory

before she moves away from the group to give birth in solitude. Twins have been seen, but a single calf is the rule. She stays alone with her new calf for a few days before she will tolerate the close presence of other rhinoceroses. In this respect, white and black rhinoceroses behave in a very similar way.

Female white rhinoceroses breed at two or three year intervals, and they can live for between 40 and 50 years: on average, a female which is allowed to live out its natural life span can produce ten or eleven calves. By comparison with other ungulates, this is a very slow rate of reproduction. However, in the natural state, the white rhinoceros is immune to predation: coupled with the highly ritualised combat which has reduced casualties by replacing open aggression, this immunity produces a very low natural mortality. This slow replacement rate was the main cause of the very rapid decline of white rhinoceros populations under pressure from European hunters.

Signs and Signals

The white rhinoceros makes a wide range of sounds, which have been given different meanings, depending on the social situations in which they are heard. The contact call between two animals meeting at a distance is a husky panting sound, rather like a cough. A juvenile whines after its mother, and squeals loudly when alarmed, perhaps by temporarily losing sight of her. The threat calls given by resident alpha males to intruders into their territories begin with a low growl, which is replaced by a fierce bellow as the threat becomes more intense. The submission sound which turns away the wrath of the alpha male has been called a chirping call; it sounds like a high-pitched growl. As the alpha becomes more energetic in his threat, the intensity of the submission call increases, until it might be described as a shriek. On the very rare occasions when fighting breaks out, it is a very noisy affair, as the threats and submissions rise through their various levels of intensity.

The wails of a courting male are often accompanied by a sound called 'hic-throbbing'; its significance is not clear, but it may have something in common with the very deep abdominal growls of elephants, which are now known to be transmitted for long distances through the ground, and detected by other elephants through their feet. A short burst of low-pitched, high intensity sound would be ideal for this purpose.

The most conspicuous signs made by rhinoceroses to each other are the scent-messages conveyed by dung-piles and urine-spraying. Their function is primarily territorial, though there is some other significance in the dung-piles which accumulate beside regularly used trails between feeding areas and watering places. It seems as if a passing animal is stimulated to defaecate by the sight or scent of such a mound, as if it were a social duty. These trailside mounds can become quite tall, because they are not kicked about by their contributors. Dung-kicking is a privilege reserved to the dominant male in a territory. The trailside mounds may serve as an indication of population density in an area, or as confirmatory signposts on a trail which may be used only every three or four days.

Territorial dung-piles, which are distributed all over the territory until there are about 15 per 0.4 sq miles (1 sq km), are recognisable because they have been kicked by the resident male. Other passing rhinoceroses often add to them in the same way as to the trailside heaps, but they do not kick. There has been a good deal of discussion of this distinctive habit of alpha males, which leaves grooves in the ground after a long period of occupation. It may simply serve to indicate to an outsider that the area through which it is passing is occupied territory, as opposed to the no man's land crossed by the regular trails.

Urine-spraying is restricted to the boundaries of territories, and is the principal mark of ownership. The sprays are emitted in two or three short bursts: a male patrolling his borders produces such markers about every five or six minutes. They have an important effect on the outcome of conflicts between the alpha bull and intruders into his territory: the intruder must be aware as soon as he has crossed the boundary that he will be the loser in any confrontation with the proprietor of the territory.

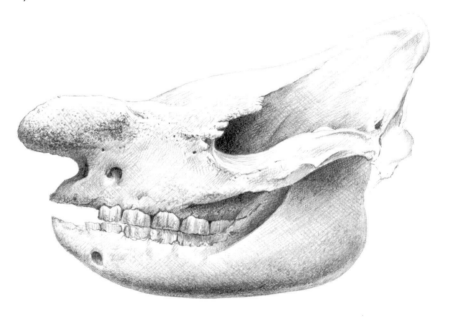

Figure 16: The skull of a white rhinoceros shows the bony boss which supports the horn

Horns

Selous shot a female white rhinoceros with a front horn measuring 108 cm (3 ft 7 in in his account), and found it worthy of comment: the record is in fact over 6 ft 6 in (2 m), but such huge horns are very rare nowadays. Probably few rhinoceroses reach a sufficient age to grow them. The females' horns are longer and thinner than those of the males.

The front horn usually has a smoothly polished and slightly flattened leading surface, from regular contact with the ground during grazing. It is sometimes used for digging, when the grass is too short to graze and the animals have to turn their attention to roots as their main source of food. It is not unknown for the horn to be torn off during digging, especially the very long thin specimens grown by females. A female in Berlin Zoo whose front horn was torn off in an accident in May 1963, had a visible bump where the horn had been by July; by December, the horn was 5 in (13 cm) long, and by March 1967 it had reached a length of $13\frac{1}{2}$ in (34.5 cm), growing at 0.2 in (0.5 cm) per month. Among the white rhinoceroses at Whipsnade Park in England there are two or three whose horns have been damaged but not removed: there is evidence of regeneration, but it is lumpy and irregular, producing some grotesquely deformed horns. For cosmetic reasons, it might have been as well if the horns had been removed when they were first damaged, so that they would have grown again in a more typical form. The thought of horn regeneration, if it always happens at the rate described for Berlin Zoo, raises the spectre of a regular source of income to zoos with tractable herds of white rhinoceroses, from selling horns which could be removed at regular intervals.

'Operation Rhino'

The white rhinoceros was considered to be extinct in 1892, only 75 years after the explorer Burchell had discovered it. However, a few individuals survived in the valley of the Umfolozi River, in Natal: when they were found, in 1897, the government of South Africa declared the valley a preserve. From then on, the population increased steadily, until in 1930 there were thought to be about 30. By 1960, the population numbered 1,500, there and in the neighbouring Hluhluwe Reserve. The area was overstocked, and there was a risk that the rhinoceroses would damage their habitat by overgrazing it. Five hundred individuals had already been shipped out to other parks, and to zoos around the world. The decision was taken to move some of the rhinoceroses to England, to form a breeding herd in Whipsnade Park, under the aegis of the Zoological Society of London.

The Natal Parks Board carried out the operation. The original plan was to dart 40 rhinoceroses and transport them by truck and ship halfway across the world. In the event, only 20 animals were moved, eight males and twelve females: but the operation was a success, and the herd at Whipsnade has produced 34 calves since 1970, of which over 20 have been sent away to other captive breeding herds, in nine different countries.

Elsewhere in South Africa, the white rhinoceros population is now at full capacity. Indeed, at Pilanesberg National Park, up to ten white rhinoceroses per year are shot by trophy-hunters, at a price of $10,000 each. Ron Thomson, the pioneering wildlife biologist, in his *On Wildlife 'Conservation'*, uses a scale of status when describing wildlife which ranges through ten grades of rarity, with endangered status at the top of the scale. (Animals going beyond 'Endangered' are extinct.)

Thomson estimates that the white rhinoceros in southern Africa has moved from Endangered status to 8 on the scale in just 50 years, and is no longer in need of protective management.

The northern race of white rhinoceros has had almost an exactly opposite fate. Since its discovery in 1907, it has suffered at the hands of white sport hunters, and later commercial poachers, until it is virtually extinct throughout its range. The Congo civil war reduced that country's population of rhinoceroses from over 1,000 to less than 100. Between 1961 and 1964, white rhinoceroses from Kenya and Uganda were darted and collected together in Murchison Falls National Park: but the upheavals in Uganda during and after the reign of Idi Amin effectively wiped out the white rhinoceros in the country. In 1979 there were said to be as many as 25 white rhinoceroses in Kabaleze National Park, but by 1980 they were all gone, as were the 80 animals reported from Ajai's Reserve, which was designated especially for the white rhinoceros. By 1986, the only remaining animals from which a new population could have been built up were the 17 individuals in Zaire. Garamba National Park is the subject of a major rehabilitation programme under the guidance of the World Wildlife Fund, for the sake of its remarkable populations of buffalo, elephant, hippopotamus and giraffe. The remaining rhinoceroses will no doubt be encouraged to expand their numbers within the Park, but there seems very little hope that they will ever re-occupy their once extensive range elsewhere in northern Africa.

6
The Great Indian One-horned Rhinoceros

▼▼▼

THE GREAT INDIAN ONE-HORNED RHINOCEROS
Scientific name: *Rhinoceros unicornis*
Common names: Great Indian one-horned rhinoceros,
Indian rhinoceros

Range and numbers (1985 figures)

INDIA
Kaziranga	1,195
Manas	75
Pabitara	67
Orang	60
Laokhowa	40
Jaldapara	20
Other locations	30
Total in 10 locations	1,487

Note: small populations are reported from six other locations in India from which there is no current estimate.

NEPAL
Chitwan	400
Bardia (1986)	4

PAKISTAN
Lal Suhanra	2
Total world population	1,893

Source: Species Conservation Monitoring Unit 1987: WWF Yearbook 1985/1986

Length of head and body	7–14 ft	(2.1–4.2 m)
Height at shoulder	$3\frac{1}{2}$–$6\frac{1}{2}$ ft	(1.1–2.0 m)
Weight	3,300–4,400 lb	(1,500–2,000 kg)
Length of horn	8–24 in	(20–61 cm)

Distribution and Status

The great one-horned rhinoceros once ranged extensively across the plain of the Ganges, from the Indus Valley in the west all the way to Assam. There are accounts of rhinoceros hunts during the reign of the Moghul Emperor Zahiruddin Mohamed Babur (1505–30), when the species was to be found right across the north of India to Peshawar, near what is now the border between Pakistan and Afghanistan. However, its population dwindled sharply during the nineteenth century, under pressure from the expanding human population, for whose crops it

▲▲▲

was a very efficient competitor. The second cause of its decline was the very heavy hunting which developed to satisfy the demand for its meat, blood and horn for medicinal and ritual uses. European hunters took a significant number during the heyday of the Raj, without ascribing any supernatural powers to the rhinoceros, but merely for the sport of killing a large, albeit inoffensive, animal.

The original wide range of the one-horned rhinoceros has contracted eastwards, until only a few reserves in northern India, and one in Nepal, continue to support it in any significant numbers.

It is fortunate that there are any left at all. It was only in 1910 that the hunting of rhinoceroses was banned in Assam and Bengal, by which time most of the survivors were to be found in Assam, apart from the separate population in the terai of southern Nepal, an area of swampy grasslands surrounded by tall forests. The first reserves to be declared, at Kaziranga and Manas, still hold the two largest populations of rhinoceroses in India. Kaziranga was promoted from a Forest Reserve to a Game Sanctuary in 1926. It was closed to all visitors, and immediately became the haunt of a large number of poachers. When Kaziranga was opened to the public in 1938, the activities of the poachers ceased; they were unable to

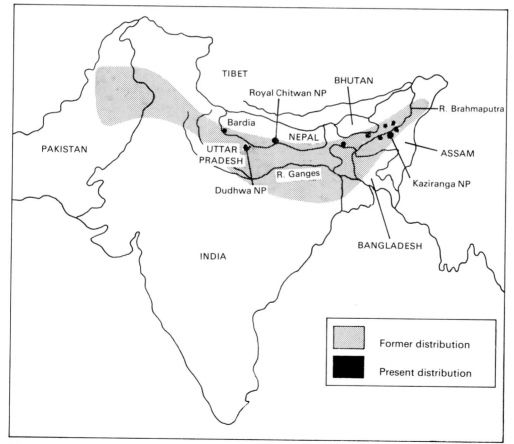

Map 4: Past and present distribution of the great one-horned Indian rhinoceros

continue their predation under the eye of a steady stream of observant, and very often official, visitors. The rhinoceros population at Kaziranga has risen nearly five-fold since a survey in 1959 by the great biologist of India, E. P. Gee: he estimated the number in the reserve at that time as 260.

The royal hunting grounds at Chitwan in Nepal became a reserve in 1973, after a survey by Gee in 1958 had shown that there were between 300 and 400 animals left. Although their numbers fell sharply thereafter — Gee's estimate in 1964 was below 185 — the success of the reserve is clear from the figures for the 1985 population, which is once more around the 400 mark.

The reasons for the success of rhinoceros conservation in Nepal were outlined in 1985 by Dr Esmond Bradley Martin, the American biologist, in *Oryx*. He pointed out that the Nepalese people who live within reach of the park are deterred from poaching not only by the presence of 500 armed men of the Royal Nepalese Army, but also by an enlightened attitude on the part of the Park authorities (which means the King of Nepal, who has absolute authority in his country). Rhinoceroses which die of natural causes within the Park are made available to the people, so that the parts of the animal which are important in religious observances may be removed and used.

The hide is used to make containers for the libations of milk and water which play a central part in the ceremony of *Shradda*, by which both Hindus and Buddhists commemorate their parents and grandparents on the anniversary of their deaths. The meat, including the liver, is used for medicinal purposes, and the dried blood is used by women to ease menstrual pain, and by men occasionally as an aphrodisiac. Rhinoceros urine may be bought at the zoo in Kathmandu, but it is often collected in the field in the form of soaked sand. It is regarded as a powerful medicine for a wide range of complaints. The bones may be used to make oil lamps for religious purposes, or rings to ward off evil spirits. The horn and hooves, which are highly regarded, are not available, since they are the property of the King. They are removed and taken away to the Palace.

The effect of this policy has been to undermine the market for poached rhinoceros products, partly because of the near certainty of being arrested and severely punished (with up to five years in prison and a fine so steep as to be unpayable, which will put the family into debt for years), and partly because such products as are really important for their religious or medical value are relatively easily available. As a result, not one rhinoceros has been poached within the Park's boundaries since 1976. This represents an enormous achievement, considering that between 1950 and Gee's estimate in 1964 the population had been reduced from 800 to about 185 animals. In 1986, four one-horned rhinoceroses (three females and one male) were removed from Royal Chitwan National Park and placed in the Royal Bardia Wildlife Reserve, in western Nepal, to form the nucleus of a new breeding group.

All the signs are that despite its much reduced range, the one-horned rhinoceros population is increasing steadily in the areas where it is now so carefully protected.

Diet

A great deal has been learned about the diet of the one-horned rhinoceros in the wild, since the first captive animal in England was fed on rice, sugar and hay, with liberal offerings of wine. Even then, in 1739, the animal's keepers noticed that it seemed fonder of fresh greens of various kinds; the diet offered to rhinoceroses in modern zoos reflects much more closely their natural food.

The one-horned rhinoceros is principally a grazing animal, moving about its feeding range to take advantage of fresh growth wherever it is to be found. Although it is usually described as a creature of swampy areas and grassy riverine plains, it will also move into drier grassland, and even into higher wooded country, especially where stream beds and ravines give it access from lower-lying land. When the newly-planted rice crop is growing, rhinoceroses from wildlife reserves often move into agricultural land to feed on the young shoots — coming into direct conflict with the neighbouring people. Other crops which are taken include corn, wheat, mustard, lentils and potatoes.

The one-horned rhinoceros is adaptable in its use of its feeding apparatus: the semi-prehensile upper lip which enables it to feed on tall grasses and slender twigs can be folded out of the way when it needs to graze on short, fresh grasses. Bamboo shoots and water hyacinth are also acceptable; in eating the latter, the rhinoceroses are doing themselves a favour, by keeping their wallows open.

Figure 17: The upper lip of the Indian rhinoceros is adaptable: it can be used to grasp bunches of grass, or tucked out of the way for grazing shorter turf

Grass

In preparing areas of reserves to increase the number of one-horned rhinoceroses they can support, and more particularly to reduce the incentive for the animals to stray into neighbouring agricultural land, managers often cut the tall elephant grass beside rivers. This encourages the growth of new grass, and attracts rhinoceroses to feed on it.

However, the cutting must be done in a restrained way, since the tall grass is not only an important feature of the habitat of the rhinoceros, offering shelter as well as food, but also the home of a very large number of other animals, including tigers. A conflict of interest has arisen on the borders of Royal Chitwan National Park, between the Park authorities and the local people. It is based partly on the people's need for long grass with which to thatch their houses: they also need short grass on which to graze their cattle. There is a clear temptation for them to enter the park to kill two birds with one stone: in removing their thatching grass they are also preparing a fresh pasture for their domestic stock.

In 1986, a total of 80,500 tons (81,812 tonnes) of grass was removed from the Park by local people. They paid a fee for the privilege of cutting it, but reports suggest that roughly 100 times more grass was taken than was paid for. Furthermore, cattle are driven into the Park almost daily to feed, competing with the rhinoceroses for the precious grass.

One suggested solution to this problem has been to transport the cut grass out of the Park, and to supply it to the people who need it as roofing material or as fodder for their cattle. The problem of cattle invading a reserve is one which is common all over the world, though in Chitwan people might be less anxious to let their stock wander inside the Park boundaries, in view of the number of tigers which flourish there.

Daily Routine

The daily routine of the one-horned rhinoceros is even more leisurely and peaceful than that of the African species, since it spends little time or energy in conflict. It spends the latter part of the afternoon in the shade of the forest, leaving for more open feeding areas as evening approaches. During the early part of the night it feeds, usually choosing an area of short turf, either where the grass is recovering from being burned or where it has been heavily grazed some time previously. The edges of rivers or pools are favoured places, where new grass is always growing on the rim of the denser stands.

Towards midnight, the rhinoceroses rest, the adults lying down in the feeding area, ready to resume grazing in the early morning. Females with young calves may retire at this time to the tall elephant grass, where the youngsters are less vulnerable to the unnoticed approach of a tiger; but a fully grown adult has no enemies, and can rest safely in relatively open terrain.

By morning, the adults begin to move into cover, grazing quietly as they go, only to emerge towards noon to go to their wallows. From midday until late afternoon, they remain almost completely submerged, in social groups of as many as nine together, adults and young in the same sleepy association.

Wallowing not only protects the rhinoceroses from the attacks of insects, and keeps their skin supple; it also prevents sunburn, and the overheating which is inevitable in such a bulky animal. The placid movements of undisturbed rhinoceroses seem as if they are designed to reduce the generation of unwanted heat. However, their movements can be very nimble when the occasion demands.

Mobility

Most hunting authors of the nineteenth century drew attention to the surprising speed and agility of the one-horned rhinoceros. Following a wounded animal through the tall grass in order to finish it off was demanded of the true sportsman; it must have been a nerve-racking ordeal for anyone who had seen the awesome spectacle of a rhinoceros at full gallop. The fact that a charge is rarely carried through would have been small consolation to a hunter, no matter how heavily armed, shouldering his way through grass 10 ft (3 m) tall, where the visibility is little more than 3 ft (1 m) at best. The pursuit had fatal results on more than one occasion; but still the one-horned rhinoceros retained its reputation as a timid, inoffensive animal, always readier to run than to fight.

Many rhinoceros hunts were undertaken on elephant back, but the security of a perch high above the ground was illusory, since Indian elephants are terrified of rhinoceroses. Training them to stand their ground in the face of a charge was considered virtually impossible: it has been one of the triumphs of the Tiger Tops lodge in Royal Chitwan National Park to produce a team of elephants which will refrain from panicking when their mahouts gather them into a half-circle around a rhinoceros, for the visitors to admire and photograph. Probably, familiarity has reduced each species' unease in the presence of the other; encounters with tourist-laden elephants have become part of the rhinoceroses' daily routine in that splendid and spectacular Park. Nevertheless, the discipline of the elephants is very apparent, as one sits on the trembling back of an elephant with a rhinoceros in full view.

Social Behaviour

The one-horned rhinoceros is not territorial in the same way as the African species. Wolfgang Ullrich, former Director of the Dresden Zoo, described the division of the grass jungle into 'public' and 'private' areas, connected by paths which also have 'public' or 'private' status. The public areas include wallows and bathing places, which are open for the use of all rhinoceroses. Private paths lead to grazing areas, about 5,000 sq yd (4,000 sq m) in extent, which are defended by individual males, females, or females with calves. Each animal also defends its own sleeping place in the elephant grass, approached by another private path.

There is no urine-spraying or aggressive patrolling to defend these areas, however. Bulls occasionally fight with intruders into their feeding area, but more often a short grunting charge is enough to settle the conflict. The females, too, fight for territory, though they more often keep their distance within their own area, as if by common consent. It is not unusual to see rhinoceroses with apparently severe wounds and old scars, produced by their opponents' sharp lower incisors during these territorial skirmishes. However, since their feeding territories are large and often out of sight of each other, confrontations are more often accidental than deliberate.

There is no evidence of the use of dung as a territorial marker, though the one-horned rhinoceros establishes and uses communal dung-heaps in the same way as its African relatives. This probably has a social function, as it were a continuously updated directory of animals present in the area. The heaps can become enormous, as much as 16 ft (5 m) across and over 3 ft (1 m) high; they are added to by every animal which passes them. There are reports of rhinoceroses pausing in full flight to defaecate on a dung-heap, which suggests that it is a social imperative of the highest order to update the directory, even more vital in times of stress than when the community is at peace. The dung-heaps are always in public, not in private places; beside wallows and bathing pools, and near the entrances to the tunnel-like public paths leading into the elephant grass. They might serve as signposts through the otherwise featureless grasslands.

Wallows are open to all comers. Seven individuals were seen leaving one pool, trotting off in different directions when they were disturbed. New arrivals at a pool are challenged by those already wallowing, answering their grunts and snorts with their own. When the wallowing animals snort back, the newcomers are able to join the party unopposed; it looks very much as if a password had been demanded, given, and accepted.

Apart from grunting and snorting in alarm or in social greeting, the one-horned rhinoceros has a limited vocabulary. Captured animals produce a bellow of panic (or rage?), and courting females, especially those observed at close quarters in zoos, make a whistling sound during the courtship chases.

Courtship and Breeding

The courtship of one-horned rhinoceroses has been observed only rarely in the wild, but frequently in zoos, especially the Basle Zoo, where one-horned rhinoceroses have been breeding successfully since 1956.

Females are sexually mature from about three years of age, and bulls from seven or nine years old. A female comes into season for 24 hours every five to eight weeks, advertising her condition by spraying urine, and uttering her strange whistling sound with every breath. The male reacts to her signals by spraying urine himself, and by chasing her; in the zoo the animals were seen to take turns in driving each other round and round their enclosure, following their exertions with long periods of rest. The female remains close to the weary bull while he is recovering his breath, until eventually he begins his attempts to mount her. The intimate signals between the partners are essentially the same as in the African black rhinoceros, with the difference that the partners bite each other gently with their incisors, instead of tussling with their horns. Mounting is preceded by the bull laying his head across the female's hindquarters, in just the same way as the black rhinoceros. Copulation lasts for an average of an hour; the longest recorded at Basle Zoo lasted for 83 minutes. When it was over, the animals paid no further attention to each other.

The gestation period is about 16 months: 12 pregnancies at Basle lasted for between 462 and 489 days. The Basle female showed signs of irritability just before the birth, becoming nervous, and making mock attacks on her keeper, whom she

Plate 7 : Wallowing is an important activity for all rhinos. Mud acts as a cooling agent and it probably also protects against parasites, as well as keeping the skin supple.

Plate 8: White rhinoceroses are not normally gregarious but they sometimes form gatherings, when a number of subadults group around a childless female, often referred to as an 'aunt'.

Plate 9: Rhinoceros mothers protect their calves against all comers. Lions very rarely manage to kill a calf: spotted hyaenas are a much greater danger.

had hitherto treated with the greatest trust and good nature. The newborn calf weighs 145 lb (65 kg), and begins at once the impressive intake of milk which enables it to gain $4\frac{1}{2}$–$6\frac{1}{2}$ lb (2–3 kg) in weight every day. The milk production of the mother is about 35–44 pints (20–25 litres) a day.

The calf has all the skin-folds of the adult when it is born, with a smooth plate on its nose where the horn will grow. One apparent difference between the African and Asian species is that the horn of the Asians is much more firmly attached to the skull, because of the greater size of the bony boss which supports it.

One of those intriguing zoological conundrums, which remind one so much of the Victorian naturalists, who went in for major controversies over the most minor of points, is the question of whether the one-horned rhinoceros calf follows or leads its mother as they move together through the bush. There is evidence for both answers, from observations in the zoo and from photographs taken in the wild: the generally accepted conclusion is that calves follow close behind their mothers while they are still small, but begin to travel in front of them as they grow larger.

The first calf born in Basle Zoo began chewing leaves at only two weeks old, but did not feed properly on hay and grass until it was nearly two months old. The age of weaning in the wild is not known.

Predators

The one-horned rhinoceros has almost no predators in the wild, though there is evidence that tigers will take young calves if they can. The mothers fight fiercely in defence of their young, using their teeth to inflict serious injuries. A nineteenth-century hunter reported following a rhinoceros which he had wounded late one afternoon: he found it the next day engaged in fighting off the attacks of two tigers, both of which were severely wounded and covered in blood. Like so many other large herbivores, the one-horned rhinoceros, with its confidence born of invulnerability in its natural habitat, falls an easy victim to the bullet.

Guggisberg, whose *S.O.S. Rhino* supplied much of the information in this chapter, quotes a touching episode from the days of the Indian Mutiny. A soldier was court-martialled for shooting a tame rhinoceros which his regiment had captured: his explanation of the offence was that he wanted to see whether the animal's hide really was bulletproof, as he had read. From the earliest days, the hide of the one-horned rhinoceros was thought to be proof against the sharpest weapons, because of its 'riveted' appearance. When dried, rhinoceros hide makes excellent shields, but while the animal is alive, its hide is as soft and supple, and as penetrable, as any other skin. The German name for the one-horned rhinoceros, *Panzernashorn*, contains the same misapprehension as Ogden Nash's rhyme:

I shoot the bold rhinoceros with bullets made of platinum,
Because if I use leaden ones, his hide is sure to flatten 'em.

As the court-martialled soldier discovered, and as many hunters have known for a long time, there is no truth in it. The one-horned rhinoceros is as easy to kill as any other slow-moving, peacable creature; and as difficult to protect from the determined human predator.

7
The Javan Rhinoceros

THE JAVAN RHINOCEROS
Scientific name: *Rhinoceros sondaicus*
Common names: Javan rhinoceros, Lesser one-horned rhinoceros
Range and numbers (1985 figures)

INDONESIA
Udjung Kulon   50

Source: Species Conservation Monitoring Unit 1987.

Length of head and body	11 ft 6 in	(3.5 m)
Height at shoulder	6 ft	(1.8 m)
Weight	3,527 lb	(1,600 kg)
Length of horn	10–10¼ in	(25–27 cm)

Distribution and Status

The distribution of the Javan rhinoceros in the past is difficult to disentangle, because the species was distinguished from the Indian one-horned rhinoceros only at the beginning of the nineteenth century. It is different in several ways: it lacks the knobbly skin which gives the one-horned rhinoceros its 'riveted' appearance, having instead a skin which looks scaly, with a pattern like a mosaic; the folds of skin across its neck are much less complex, and those on the shoulders join in the midline of the back, giving the animal a segmented look, more like an armadillo; and the horn is small and restricted to the males. Females have nothing more than a small knob in place of a horn.

Accounts of a one-horned rhinoceros in Java during the seventeenth century were assumed to refer to the Indian species, whose range was therefore thought to extend into the Malay Archipelago. The difference between the species was observed by several zoologists of the early 1800s, and formalised in 1822 with the necessary technical description by the French zoologist Desmarest. Confusion continued, however, when the Javan species was found to occur also in Sumatra, as well as historically through Burma into Assam and Bengal. The two species lived side by side on the mainland, in Burma, Malaya, Thailand, most of Indochina and south-western China. Even as late as 1971, the zoologist S. H. Prater, in his *Book of Indian Animals*, included the 'smaller one-horned, or Javan rhinoceros', though he remarks that it is extinct from India and Burma, adding that 'It is possible, though not very likely, that the species may still exist in some of the more remote and ill-explored tracts of the Malay Peninsula'.

The decline of the Javan rhinoceros was very rapid. Its cause was not only poaching: in the mid-eighteenth century the rhinoceroses were so numerous that they caused serious damage to crops, inspiring the government of the time to offer a high bounty to hunters who would kill them: 526 were accounted for in two years. In the rest of their range, hunting for medicinal purposes may have been more important, though competition with agriculture was the principal reason for the enmity of humans. At any rate, soon after it was discovered by Western science, the

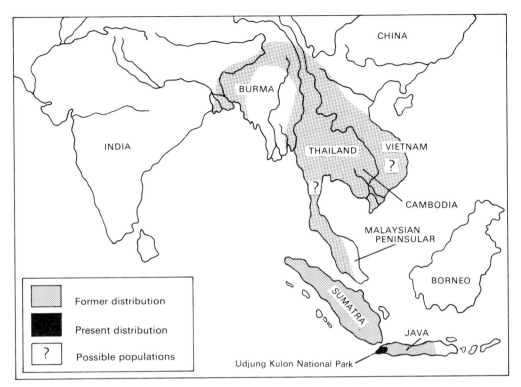

Map 5: Past and present distribution of the Javan rhinoceros

species was becoming scarce. The French explorer and big game hunter, Edmond de Poncins, writing in 1892, tracked down a small group of rhinoceroses in the Sunderbans. He was surprised to find that they were the Javan species, having expected to find the Indian; but having identified them he left them alone, since 'they had no trophy worth having, and shooting them was without excuse'. He knew, however, that poaching was very common in the area, and it is possible that the rhinoceroses he spared were wiped out not long afterwards.

The last specimen shot in Burma was collected for the British Museum in 1920, and the last known from Malaya was shot in Perak, again as a museum specimen, in 1932. The species became extinct in Sumatra in the mid-1940s, having been relatively common there until the end of the last century. There were rumours of surviving rhinoceroses in South Vietnam in the early 1960s, but none was ever confirmed. Most zoologists now conclude, sadly, that the only place where the species survives is in the Udjung Kulon National Park, at the western tip of Java, where the latest estimate of the population is 50 animals. However, the population is very healthy, with balanced numbers of young males and adult females, and in the 1984 census the researchers found the prints of three newly-weaned calves.

Diet

The Javan rhinoceros is a browsing animal, a forest inhabitant whose original wide range was made possible by its catholic diet. It feeds on a variety of trees and shrubs, bending saplings over until it can reach the leaves at the crown, often grasping them with its prehensile upper lip, similar to that of the African browsing species, the black rhinoceros. It will also feed from low-hanging branches and from bushes. It has been found in forested hill country at over 6,500 ft (2,000 m) above sea level, the altitude described as its 'usual habitat'. In his field study of this species, carried out for the World Wildlife Fund in 1967, Professor Rudolf Schenkel found it feeding in the sparse forests of the mountainous parts of the reserve, where openings produced by fallen trees encouraged the growth of young saplings, and also at the edge of coastal forests at sea level at the southern edge of the park.

The American zoologist, Lee Talbot, reporting on a visit to Java in 1959, observed that the Javan rhinoceros ate twigs and fruit as well as leaves. He saw trees as much as $3\frac{1}{2}$ in (9 cm) in diameter being pushed over by the animals, which would lean on the trunk and then walk over the tree, forcing it down between their forelegs until they could reach the parts which they wished to eat. He also saw rhinoceroses eating young bamboos, and heard a report of one which was standing in the sea, apparently eating mangroves.

Some Biological Notes

Very little more is known about the biology of the Javan rhinoceros. What follows is a summary garnered from the three or four authors who have written about the species at first hand or from direct reports.

The only account of the reproductive biology of the Javan rhinoceros, in *National Geographic* for June 1985, gives the age for sexual maturity of females as three years,

Figure 18. The similarity between the Javan and Indian rhinoceroses (they are members of the same genus) led to confusion until the species were separated in 1822

and for males as 'about twice that'. The rut is said to occur sporadically and non-seasonally, accompanied by 'frightful roaring and aggressive behaviour by bulls'. Gestation is given as 16 months, and the cow is said to remain with the calf for about two years. This information was provided by Dieter Plage, the wildlife cameraman, who managed to film the animals in 1981.

Talbot describes an encounter with a cow and her calf during his first survey. He was stalking rhinoceroses in the company of the Director of Udjung Kulon National Park, Mr Soekardi, and some Javanese assistants.

We had been following their tracks when we caught sight of the baby disappearing into the jungle some yards ahead. The carriers and trackers promptly and prudently took to the trees, as they always did when we came to a rhino. Mr Soekardi and I pushed ahead and crawling round a clump of rattan, we unexpectedly came upon the little rhino at a distance of about [16 feet] five metres. It was chewing tepus *(Nicolaia sp.)*, a favourite food of the rhino. Soon it lay down, first folding its hind legs and sitting with its front legs stiff, looking around. Then it folded its front legs also and laid its head down on the ground. This jungle is so dense that even at that range our view was not very clear, for although it was early afternoon, the jungle floor was very dark. Suddenly the mother rhino stepped from behind a rattan clump and stood beside the baby looking at us. She stared for a long time, blinking her black eyes, swinging her head, sniffing with flaring nostrils, and flicking her ears. We were down wind, exactly five metres from her tracks. She suddenly jumped back about two steps, turned and began calmly feeding. Shortly thereafter the baby got up and the two moved away.

Other naturalists, and Talbot himself on other occasions, have reported that Javan rhinoceroses ran away as soon as they became aware of the presence of a human being. Evidently they have rather poor eyesight, since they were unable to recognise Talbot as a human being at a range of 5 yd (4.5 m) until they got his scent, whereupon they would snort and dash away upwind.

There are several accounts of attacks on humans by alarmed rhinoceroses. Some of them had evidently been passed down by word of mouth to Talbot's porters from the time when the species was much more common. Groups of porters have been charged and their baggage trampled, and one Dutch naturalist was tossed and badly bitten by a Javan rhinoceros which he surprised in thick cover.

The density of the jungle has prevented better observation of the species. Its tracks were at one time easy to find, consisting of deep grooves in the ground, covered by a low green tunnel where the animals had pushed repeatedly through the vegetation. One nineteenth-century explorer noted that local travellers would find and follow a rhinoceros track when they needed water; the tracks almost invariably led to a spring or a pool in the forest. The tracks were used by the pioneers who opened up the remoter parts of Java, and it is said that many of the roads on the island were originally surveyed and laid out by rhinoceroses.

As well as being a useful pathfinder in the dense forest, the Javan rhinoceros is an agile climber. The nineteenth-century German naturalist Junghuhn found them among the highest mountains, and even on the rim of active volcanoes.

During his survey of the rhinoceroses in Udjung Kulon, Schenkel saw the males spraying bushes with urine, orange-red in colour, which he said 'smells like horse urine'. This at least explained the origin of the red splashes on bushes in the forest, which had been thought to be produced from a nasal gland. These scent-marks may have a territorial function, or serve to identify a passing bull to those which follow him along the track. The Javan rhinoceros does not apparently use dung as a marker in the same way as other species. Schenkel observed that they sometimes defaecate in creeks, or at other times in regular dung-fields, as much as 33 ft (10 m) across; at other times they simply drop their dung as they walk along the trail. He concluded that to the Javan rhinoceros dung is not especially important for communication within the species.

Conservation

The population of Javan rhinoceroses in Udjung Kulon has been estimated at various times in recent years. Talbot's first survey in 1959 produced an estimate of between 24 and 45 individuals; but the difficulty of spotting the extremely secretive animals, and the frequency of their criss-crossing tracks in the jungle, make accurate counts of the species very difficult. On a repeat visit in 1964, Talbot came to a total of 56 individuals, but failed to find any evidence of young animals. He pointed out in his report that in the previous ten years six young rhinoceroses had been reported, and about a dozen had died or been killed. Without being able to ascribe a reason for its decline, he formed a very pessimistic opinion of the species' chances of survival.

The latest available estimate of the population is from a PhD thesis by Nico van Strien in 1985. He came to a total of 50 animals; but within the evident margin of error produced by the density of the cover and the secretive behaviour of the animals this only indicates that the numbers remain substantially unchanged since 1964. The only factor which has changed in the last 20 years has been the final disappearance of the Javan tiger, which is now officially regarded as extinct. In 1966, there were about a dozen tigers left. They constituted a minor threat to the survival of the rhinoceros, since a tiger would be able to kill a calf which had become separated from its mother.

The story is often quoted of how the tiger saved the rhinoceros after the end of the Second World War. Apparently a gang of poachers decided to enter the reserve in order to slaughter the remaining rhinoceroses for their horns. They abandoned their enterprise when one of their number was killed by a tiger. Now that the tigers have gone, the only remaining threat to the rhinoceros, apart from the sparseness of its small population, is human predation.

8
The Sumatran Rhinoceros

▼▼▼

THE SUMATRAN RHINOCEROS
Scientific name: *Didermoceros sumatrensis*
Common names: Sumatran rhinoceros, two-horned Asian rhinoceros

Range and numbers (1985 figures)

Burma (2 locations)	10–11
Indonesia (4 locations)	405–760
Malaysia (12 locations)	68–106
Total in 3 countries	483–877

Source: Species Conservation Monitoring Unit 1987.

Length of head and body	8–9 ft	(2.5–2.8 m)
Height at shoulder	3–5 ft	(1.0–1.5 m)
Weight	2,200 lb	(1,000 kg)
Length of front horn	10–31 in	(25–80 cm)

Distribution and Status

The Sumatran rhinoceros had a very wide distribution until the end of the last century. It was found in Bengal and Assam, all over Burma and in the hill country of Thailand, in Cambodia, Vietnam and Laos, and in Malaya, Borneo and Sumatra. Its range overlapped that of the Javan rhinoceros, except in Java itself. It has been the subject of intensive hunting for centuries, because of the value of its horn, and it is now well on the way to extinction.

The surviving populations in Indonesia are the strongest and best protected, especially in the reserves at Kerinci, with between 250 and 500 animals at the last estimate, and Gunung Leuser, where between 130 and 200 survive. The populations of Burma and Malaysia are too small to survive naturally, with the possible exception of one group of 20–25 animals. There is no recent estimate of the populations of Laos, Vietnam or Thailand, but there is no reason to suppose that a single individual survives in any of those countries.

The sudden decline of the species is all the more tragic because almost nothing is known about its biology. It is universally agreed to be the oldest rhinoceros, in evolutionary terms, as shown by its relatively hairy coat, especially pronounced in young animals, and the fringe of hairs around its ears. Otherwise, the details of its way of life are mainly to be found in the curt notes of hunters and travellers, most of whom saw the species when it was relatively abundant.

Some Biological Notes

The Sumatran rhinoceros is usually described as solitary, though males and females have sometimes been seen together, presumably during the courtship and mating season. Individuals spend the hot part of the day and the middle of the

▲▲▲

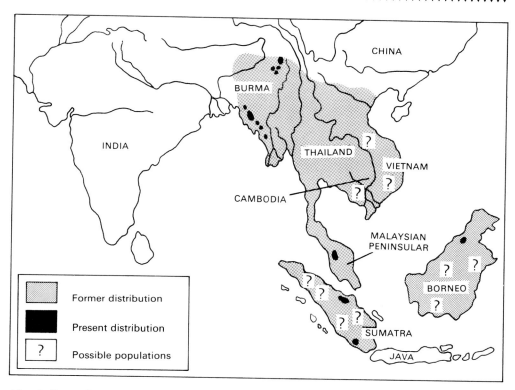

Map 6: Past and present distribution of the Sumatran rhinoceros

night wallowing or concealed in a sheltered place, emerging in the evening and again in the early morning, usually covered in mud, to feed. With its prehensile upper lip, similar to that of the Javan rhinoceros, the Sumatran species browses on leaves, twigs, bamboo shoots, and fruits such as wild mangoes and figs. The species has been seen to eat lichens or fungus off a rotting tree, and occasionally to graze on tall grass. As they grow older, and their teeth become more worn, individuals may choose to feed on thinner twigs, making up their diet with fruit. Again like the Javan species, the Sumatran has been seen 'walking down' small trees in order to get at the leaves and fruits near their crowns.

The description of the tunnels made through the vegetation by this species, makes them sound very like those made by the Javan rhinoceros. Theodore Hubback, in a study which he made of the Sumatran rhinoceros in Malaya at the turn of the century, found paths worn deeply into limestone, with boulders which blocked the way polished smooth by the passage of the animals. He found no accumulations of dung, such as are common in some other species; but another researcher reported that in Burma dung-heaps $27\frac{1}{2}$ in (70 cm) high and 5 ft (1.5 m) across were common where the animals were not unduly disturbed.

Hubback also remarks on the roughness of the terrain and the density of the cover frequented by an animal which he was trying to follow. In particular, he describes how the animal seemed to seek out the thorniest and thickest vegetation as soon as it was aware that it was being followed.

The country he frequented was not high but extremely steep and covered with thorns of many sorts. The worst obstruction was a palm (*Calamus castaneus*), called chuchor by the Malays. It grows in dense clumps to a height of about ten feet, and is very thorny. This palm jungle was interspersed with rattans of several varieties and most of the terrain followed by this rhino, when it was alarmed, was along steep hillsides heavily wooded and covered with chuchor.

Hubback followed this individual for a total of 40 days, in five separate expeditions. He heard him three times, and came very close to him several times, but never saw him.

The Sumatran rhinoceros is an expert climber, able to go where elephants and gaur antelopes would be unable to follow, through the thickest bush and up slopes too steep for a man to climb except on all fours. The highest set of tracks of the Sumatran rhinoceros were found at over 6,500 ft (2,000 m) in Sumatra; in Burma it is known to occur regularly at nearly 5,000 ft (1,400 m).

Senses and Voices

The difficulties of studying this species even when it was common were evidently considerable. Quite apart from its mobility and love of impenetrable and difficult terrain, its senses of smell and hearing are very acute, though its eyesight is said to be poor, as befits a forest animal with limited horizons. The voices of the Sumatran rhinoceros seem more varied than those of other species, though nothing like so thorough a study has been made of the meaning of any sounds which it makes. It snorts when disturbed, and brays like a donkey when it is alarmed. While it is walking calmly, it is said to squeak, and in the wallow it snorts, grunts and blows, and also makes what has been called 'a low, plaintive, humming noise, more like something that might be produced by a bird or a gibbon'. It is sad to think that humanity has exerted itself to such an extent to wipe out one of the few animal species, other than Man, which sings in its bath.

Breeding

Grzimek mentions a Sumatran rhinoceros held in Copenhagen Zoo in 1967, which was then the only one in captivity. He also draws attention to the ironic fact that the first rhinoceros born in captivity was a Sumatran, at Calcutta Zoo in 1889. Another was born there in 1895, and the two of them eventually became part of Barnum and Bailey's menagerie. There was a time when a substantial captive population could have been built up from zoo-bred animals, but since then the species has been thought to be too rare to risk captive breeding. However, the population in Sabah, North Borneo, particularly in and around the Tabin Wildlife Reserve, now seems stable enough to be able to provide the basis of a breeding stock. Discussions have been going on since 1983, but as yet the government committee involved has come to no conclusion.

What little is known about the breeding of this species comes from those captive births in Calcutta Zoo at the end of the last century. Ernest Walker, in his encyclopaedic *Mammals of the World*, says that one young per birth is the usual number, and gives the gestation period as seven to eight months. However, it has been pointed out that this figure comes from an account of the birth of a Sumatran rhinoceros on a ship in the Port of London in 1782, and has been widely quoted ever since. A more realistic estimate by Maurice Burton, based on the animal's size and weight, is 510 to 550 days. Walker cites the slow rate of reproduction as one of the main factors in the decline of the Sumatran rhinoceros, coupled with very heavy poaching to supply the medical market.

Hunting and Trade

A Dutch officer, stationed in Sumatra before the First World War, was told by his tracker that the hunters of his father's generation rarely shot their quarry, but killed rhinoceroses by laying traps for them at steep parts of their trails. Sharply pointed stakes embedded in the ground were the favoured method, though pits dug in the rhinoceroses' well-marked trails were also used. In Borneo, the hunters fired poisoned darts from blowpipes, often after following a single rhinoceros for weeks; it seems that, then as now, rhinoceros hunting was a way of life with a substantial reward for the successful hunter.

The evidence suggests that the trade in Sumatran rhinoceroses for medicinal purposes is very old, going back centuries, if not a thousand years in Borneo and China. It has been said that protection in Malaysia is impossible, because of the number of Chinese who live in that country: however, the latest estimates of the

Figure 19: The hairy coat and fringed ears of the Sumatran rhinoceros show it to be a very old species, in evolutionary terms

populations in Indonesia give hope that at least two of the protected groups might be large enough to survive without artificial assistance, provided that their sanctuaries are proof against further disruption.

Apart from centuries of professional hunting for sale, and sport hunting by Europeans until the early years of this century, a further cause of the decline of the species has been the rate of destruction of its habitat by the timber industry and the establishment of rubber plantations. Early accounts of the species describe it as an animal often seen in open country, but possibly as a result of unrelenting persecution it has become exclusively a forest animal, ranging the hills in the densest cover, usually near streams, where the forest is tallest. As the remaining forest has been removed or degraded, its last hope of survival in many areas has gone.

A joint project in Sabah, between the World Wildlife Fund and IUCN in 1979–81, came to the encouraging conclusion that the Sumatran rhinoceros can live and breed in forest which has been selectively logged, rather than clear-felled. Poaching and agricultural clearance have been the main reasons for its decline: carefully planned selective clearance should actually help the species, by providing more food plants in the forest. However, as the World Wildlife Fund Yearbook points out, thinning the forest makes it easier for poachers to get in and out, with consequent risks to the rhinoceroses. Where the forest has been cleared, within Tabin Reserve, two new patrol vehicles have been provided for the rangers, to discourage poaching.

9

The Medical Uses of Rhinoceros Products

John A. Hunter, who may claim the sad record for having killed the highest number of rhinoceros, shredded rhinoceros horn and made it into a dark brown tea. 'Even though I drank several portions of the brew', he writes, 'I am sorry to say that I did not feel any reaction whatsoever, perhaps because I did not believe in it, or maybe because I was not in the right company.' The possible medicinal effect of the horn has recently been carefully tested, thanks to the initiative of A. Schaurte. There, too, not the slightest effect could be demonstrated. Perhaps the Asiatic superstition is based on the fact that the great Indian rhinoceros do copulate for about one hour during which the great bull ejaculates approximately every three minutes. To become capable of such sexual prowess seems to be desirable to many Asiatic people.

(Erich Thenius, in *Animal Life Encyclopaedia*)

It is tempting for people in the West to deride the faith placed by traditional Asian medicine in the use of extracts and ointments made from parts of animals. Most Europeans base their condemnation on the belief that rhinoceros horn is used exclusively as an aphrodisiac all over Asia and the Far East. At the same time, many of them may have been brought up to rub goose fat on their chests, or to eat fish for the sake of their brains, even if they were born too late to benefit from the many other traditional remedies involving eating freshly-killed spiders.

I can remember being embarrassed by warts on my fingers when I was a child. I was a willing assistant in the rituals which were supposed to cure them, though in retrospect they smack strongly of witchcraft. One involved burying a piece of bacon rind after tying it for the night to the offending finger. It had no effect. In the end, the warts vanished unnoticed, as warts often do.

As I recall, the method which 'caused' this desirable result was to read an advertisement in the *Daily Telegraph* which invited sufferers to write on a piece of paper the number of their warts, and to post the paper to a given address. When I looked for the warts to count them, they were gone. Since then, I have advised warty people to count their blemishes, as a certain cure. If the bacon rind method had worked, I should still be recommending that.

The fact that such an apparently irrational cure has survived into the twentieth century, in our supposedly scientific society, indicates that over the years it must have worked for a large enough number of people. Eastern medicine is based on centuries of trial and error, with the successes being passed down to following generations. It is very difficult to dismiss it as 'superstition' when it is supported by such a large body of evidence, even if we find it impossible to understand from the viewpoint of our particular philosophy.

There are shelves of books advocating this cure and that for this and that intractable condition. Since Eastern philosophy became fashionable in the West, the books have multiplied. People who otherwise seem quite rational drink ginseng tea or brews made from the leaves or flowers of other exotic plants. If their condition improves, whether or not it would have done so by itself, the latest effort is hailed as the only successful treatment. However, many doctors will tell you that a very large number of distressing but not life-threatening conditions will clear up of their own accord, given time and a minimum of interference.

I do not mean to deride homeopathic medicine, or meditation, or any other attempt to cure conditions which Western 'scientific' medicine has found it hard to tackle. Instead, I mean to draw attention to the function of faith in the treatment of disease. It is becoming accepted even in the West that the attitude of mind of the patient is an important factor in attaining a cure. Anything, including apparently irrational courses of treatment, which tends to produce a positive attitude in the patient is a step in the right direction.

From this starting point, it is possible to understand something of the importance of animal products in Eastern medicine. In the long run, the only way to reduce the appalling destruction of rhinoceroses, which is caused by the steady demand for their products for medical purposes, may be to convince people that they are worth conserving as a source of curative drugs. However, there is such a demand, and prices are so high even for today's tiny doses, that this may be impossible. Conservationists talk of persuading governments to work slowly and patiently at educating their peoples into another view of diseases, their causes and their cures. By the time this has achieved anything, it might well be too late to save any of the most endangered species of rhinoceros.

We must take into account the range of diseases and conditions for which rhinoceros products are believed to be a cure. In this brief survey, I am indebted to Dr Esmond Bradley Martin's book, *Rhino Exploitation*, which he wrote after a series of field visits to the East between 1980 and 1983. He found that the healing properties of rhinoceros products were viewed differently in the different countries which he visited.

Rhinoceros Medicine in India

In India, the horn is valued medically only in the Unani school of medicine, practised by Muslims. The Hindu Ayurvedic school uses almost no animal products.

Among the numerous and widely advertised love potions on sale there are indeed some based on rhinoceros products. However, they are not as common now

Plate 10: A white rhino calf nurses from its mother for more than a year. During this time, the calf can be fiercely possessive, attacking potential mates which approach its mother.

Plate 11: Oxpeckers are the constant companions of both species of African rhino. They remove external parasites and also serve as an alarm system, especially at the approach of humans.

Plate 12: The northern white rhinoceros is now restricted to Garamba National Park, Zaire, where no more than twenty individuals survive.

Plate 13: The Indian rhinoceros population has two principal nuclei, one here at Royal Chitwan National Park, Nepal and the other at Kaziranga National Park in India.

as they were in the past, not from any change in beliefs, but because the price has risen beyond the reach of all but the wealthiest members of society.

In most of the preparations offered for sale, the ground horn is mixed with herbs, in one case only one part horn to six of herbs. The mixture is taken internally, usually twice daily, stirred into some palatable vehicle such as butter or honey. Dr Martin offers no conclusions as to whether it has any effect: but from the price which wealthy people are prepared to pay for the mixture (he quotes $313 per kilo (approximately 2 lb)), they evidently believe in it.

Another medical use for rhinoceros horn was in the treatment of haemorrhoids. It involved burning the horn under the patient, who was seated on a chair with a large hole in the seat. Dr Martin reports that this treatment is rarely practised today. One imagines that it would require a large amount of horn, which would make it too expensive for all but the worst-afflicted and wealthiest patients. This may have been a reason for seeking out cheaper and less unpleasant treatments. It sounds like one of those cures which is worse than the disease.

Other conditions for which rhinoceros horn is occasionally used include arthritis and lumbago, and even polio. This last disease might seem to offer a fingerhold for the medical authorities in their attempts to persuade people away from using rhinoceros products, since there is a massive body of evidence to show that polio can be prevented by vaccination, and cannot be treated by any means. However, the evidence is only from Western medical science. It cannot be expected to convince people who believe that those in the West are radically wrong in their approach to medicine.

The use of the horn as a treatment for lumbago is a bad sign. Of the four commonest afflictions of the aging male — piles, baldness, impotence and a bad back — we have now seen rhinoceros horn being suggested as a treatment for three. Perhaps because the Indian rhinoceros is not noticeably hirsute, it has not seemed a suitable source of hair restorer.

Other rhinoceros products play a part in Unani medicine. Small strips of skin, made into rings, are worn for luck and to keep away bad spirits. (It occurs to me that some of my readers might wear an elephant-hair bangle, or carry a lucky penny.) In the old days, such rhinoceros hide rings were thought to be one of several possible cures for piles.

The blood, faeces and urine of the rhinoceros have their uses, too. Treatments based on these products are less destructive, since collecting even blood need not involve the death of the animal. Faeces and urine are sold by some Indian zoos, as treatments for a range of disorders from bumpy skin to stiff necks. The treatment for a stiff neck, according to Dr Martin's informant, is to rub it with the faeces mixed with eucalyptus oil. This can be compared with the treatment for stiff joints and muscles in Western countries, where aromatic oils are sold in various combinations, to be rubbed on to the afflicted part. Doctors repeatedly remark that any other lubricant would be just as effective, since it is the rubbing which eases the pain, not the warming feeling caused by the oil; but their remarks fall on deaf ears, as each sufferer swears by his own favourite liniment or embrocation. Again, this gives an idea of how difficult it would be to demonstrate to the Indian patient that he is wrong and Westerners are right. If athletes in the West persist in using horse-oils of one kind or another, they are in no position to tell the aching Asian that the rhinoceros dung in his particular rubbing mixture adds nothing to its effect.

The list of uses for rhinoceros urine is headed by its aphrodisiac value (it is used externally), but it includes the treatment of coughs and sore throats. So long as rhinoceroses continue to be kept in Indian zoos, there seems little harm in the continued use of their by-products, whether or not Westerners perceive any good in it.

However, Dr Martin ends his account by reporting that Muslim doctors have a use for the fat and stomach of rhinoceroses, for treating polio and skin diseases respectively. The fat is for sale at only $1.25 for 0.3 oz (10 g): though since it is used by being rubbed on to the affected limbs, it must presumably be bought in fairly large quantities, and therefore only by the relatively wealthy.

The most significant factor in the whole subject of the medical uses of rhinoceros products in India is geographical: the principal places in which they are still regarded as potent are the State of Gujarat, and Bombay, both of which have long-established connections with East Africa. Most of the supplies are smuggled across the Indian Ocean, as they have been for centuries, alongside legitimate trade goods. Thus the demand for rhinoceros products for medical purposes in India is a factor in the conservation of African rhinoceroses.

Indonesian Rhinoceros Medicine

Although the native inhabitants have their own tradition of using rhinoceros

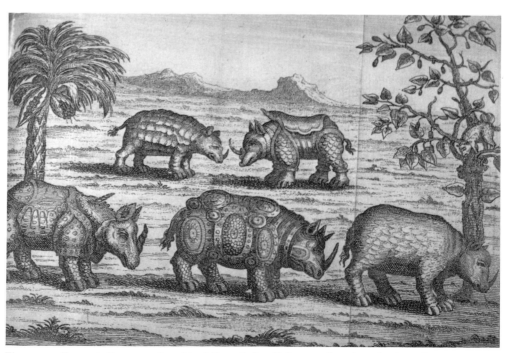

Figure 20: François Leguat, who visited Batavia in 1698, reproduced a selection of contemporary artists' impressions, with a comment mocking their fanciful embellishments

products for medicinal purposes, the demand from them is small compared with that from the Chinese, who are the principal consumers in Indonesia. They are a minority in the country, but because most of them are successful businessmen, their influence is out of proportion to their numbers. Their trust in the healing properties of the rhinoceros goes back over a thousand years; furthermore, they have the money to buy the products, a fact which is recognised and exploited by the middlemen who dispose of the poachers' victims. The principal item in their pharmacopoeia is the horn.

There is some evidence that the trade is not as widespread as it once was. In Dr Martin's survey of 26 medicine shops in Djakarta, for instance, he found only seven which were selling rhinoceros horn, and in two of those the material was in the form of shavings imported from Hong Kong. The average price of shavings which could be proved to be genuine, being prepared in front of the customer by scraping an intact Asian horn, worked out at $12,634 per kilo. The price of the imported material was only $215 per kilo. From this, Martin deduces that the imported shavings are probably not from rhinoceros horns at all. The customers must be aware of this at some level of consciousness, but they nevertheless persist in buying the cheaper article.

However, customers who are prepared to pay for it can still obtain the genuine article. Asian horn, especially that of the Javan rhinoceros, is considered far more efficacious than African horn, even in the tiny doses which are prescribed by local Chinese doctors: about 2 grams at a time. It is regarded as a very powerful drug. The horn shavings are boiled in water, which is then strained off and given to the patient to drink. It is regarded as a cure for high fever, especially typhus, and as a means of 'clearing the body of poisons'.

Rhinoceros horn is an ingredient in medicines for other complaints, such as laryngitis and deficient eyesight. More than half of the shops which Martin visited offered for sale preparations purporting to contain horn, but it would be reasonable to assume that not many of them were made from the real thing.

An occasional substitute for horn is shavings from the hoof, which are cheaper. A 3 grams dose costs about 60 cents; it is used as a drug to control fever.

The hide of the rhinoceros is also highly regarded as a medicine by the Chinese, mostly for skin diseases. It is used in much the same way as the horn, but in larger doses: the patient drinks the water in which 10 or 20 grams have been boiled. In the same way as horn can be sold in processed form, the trade in hide includes imported ready-cut strips, which sell for less than one-tenth of the price of strips cut from a skin while the customer is watching. The imported material, from Hong Kong, is often in fact water buffalo hide.

In one shop which Martin visited, in Denpasar, the capital of the island of Bali, the proprietor showed him a piece of the hide of a Javan rhinoceros which he had bought only a year previously , in 1980. He was selling it, in 0.4 oz (11 g) doses, for just under $5.00 a time. His was the only pharmacy in town, serving the 5,000 Chinese who remain on the island. That he should consider it worthwhile to stock it at all when his clientele was so small indicates that it is more than an occasional prescription.

The footnote to Martin's Indonesian survey is that while it is illegal to possess or sell any part of any species of rhinoceros in that country, there are shops in every town with a Chinese community of any size which openly offer rhinoceros products for sale. The authorities are aware of the infringements, but take no action, although the government of Indonesia ratified CITES, the Convention on International Trade in Endangered Species, in 1978.

There is a double standard in operation here, of a positively Oriental subtlety: a dealer who sells preparations containing or purporting to contain rhinoceros products is within the law, or at least not liable for prosecution, because the ingredients cannot be identified with certainty. On the other hand, presumably, he cannot be prosecuted for selling under false pretences, for the same reason.

The Chinese in Malaysia

The large cities of Malaysia have substantial Chinese populations: in Kuala Lumpur and Georgetown they are in the majority. Consequently, there is a strong demand for traditional Chinese medicines. However, since the authorities are much more vigilant and active than they are in Indonesia, only very few shops sell rhinoceros horn. They deal chiefly in imported material bought in from Hong Kong, most of it probably of African origin. The high-quality Asian horn, prepared in front of the customer, is practically unobtainable. In spite of this, the prices are, according to Martin, the highest in the world. This is partly because of the risk involved in selling any rhinoceros horn, but partly also a reflection of the wealth of the Chinese community.

It is also an indication of the deep-seated nature of the belief in rhinoceros products among Malaysia's Chinese: with full access to every Western drug and treatment for their ailments, they persist in using their own traditional medicine, with all that it implies for the fate of the rhinoceros, and indeed for the many other wild animals involved. The continuing trust in Chinese medicine cannot be shrugged off as a quirk of the Oriental mind, or as ignorance or superstition.

An international traveller in a Savile Row suit carrying in his Gucci briefcase a bottle of rhinoceros-horn pills in case of fever is not a figure of fun. He is, rather, a cause for concern. His reply to any criticism of his medical beliefs, however sympathetically offered or seriously intended, might well be to deride the traveller beside him who relies instead on aspirin, a synthetic chemical made to resemble a decoction of willow bark. The principal difference between the two medical philosophies, from the Chinese point of view, is that Westerners have identified and synthesised the active ingredients in their potions, whereas Chinese physicians and their patients place their trust in the use of unadulterated ingredients, tradition, and a long record of past success.

The depth of that trust is what threatens the remaining rhinoceroses. First-quality horn in Kuala Lumpur's Chinatown retails, on average, at $25,810 per kilo: even ready-made shavings of dubious origin go for $24,465. Outside Chinatown, the prices are lower, but at $8,971 and $2,800 respectively, they are still frighteningly high, making poaching and smuggling to supply the market a financially worthwhile risk.

In his survey of the uses of the hide of the rhinoceros in medicine in Malaysia, Martin found that only processed, pre-cut hide was for sale in Kuala Lumpur. The prices varied according to the location of the traders within the city, suggesting that they were dictated by the amount of money available rather than by any inherent value in the product. Where the hide had been prepared locally, the prices ranged from $183 to $489 per kilo: imported hide from Hong Kong sold at about $35 per kilo. He estimated that at least 70 per cent of the hide was from water-buffalo rather than rhinoceroses, including that which was processed locally.

The traders whom Martin interviewed suggested to him that the customers must know that they are being deceived, especially when they buy the cheapest products. Whether or not they know it, they take considerable quantities of water-buffalo hide in the place of rhinoceros hide, for a variety of ailments. Because they dislike the smell it produces when it is boiled in water, they cook it with pork, and often add other ingredients for particular conditions.

Another fingerhold for the conservation lobby appears here. If, after trials and sufficiently impressive results, it could be shown that water-buffalo or cow hide had effected as many cures as rhinoceros hide, the customers might be persuaded that the one was as effective as the other. An interesting offshoot from this research could be that Western sufferers from fevers and skin diseases might begin to use the by-products of the abattoir to ease their complaints, if research among the Chinese community showed that there was anything in water-buffalo hide treatment which made it as effective as the use of synthetic drugs.

Rhinoceros products are used in a similar way in Georgetown, and for the same range of complaints, though Martin reports small differences in the way in which they are prepared; they are often cooked with sugar, rather than pork, for example. He gathered some evidence to suggest that the vigilance of the government, which had an effect in raising prices in Kuala Lumpur, would be even more beneficial in other cities, where disposable incomes are lower, and there is generally not so much money available.

Raising prices by increasing the risks to poachers, smugglers and dealers is a dangerous policy to follow, unless it is carried out very firmly and extremely fast. While the price is escalating towards the point at which no one will buy the products, it will go through a wide zone in which the profits to poacher and middleman alike become so huge as to render futile any efforts at protection in the field. Although Chinese medicine is at present nowhere near as lucrative as the trade in dagger handles, it could become so, even if only for a short period. It will not take long to exterminate the few remaining Javan rhinoceroses, provided the money is right.

Before Western readers feel too self-righteous, it would be salutary to reflect on the effects of recent enlightened legislation in Britain to protect the native bird population by banning the collecting of eggs and nests. Although a majority of ex-collectors disposed of their egg collections to museums, for others the hobby was transformed overnight into big business, with enormous profits justifying the risk of imprisonment. The demand for the illicit eggs, and the money to buy them, came not from people who were concerned with anything as vital as their health, but from those who were merely following a hobby.

The Burmese Experience

An example of what might happen if the price of rhinoceros products moves beyond the reach of people's purchasing power is to be seen in Burma, where the same effect was achieved by different means. The purchasing power of the currency suddenly fell below the price of rhinoceros horn. The socialist takeover in 1962 resulted in a massive drop in the average income of the people, especially Chinese and Indian shopkeepers. The result is described in an interesting chapter of Dr Martin's book. It is encouraging in one way, and depressing reading in another.

In the only remaining Chinese medicine shop in Rangoon, there was no rhinoceros horn for sale in 1981, because the supply had run out. The proprietors had refused to buy a small amount of horn which was offered to them later because it was too expensive. Dried rhinoceros blood is sold as a tonic for people with 'weak blood', but it too is expensive, and many customers make do with what is openly called 'artificial dried rhino blood'. Similarly, 'processed' (that is, probably non-rhinoceros) hide is the only kind available for the treatment of fever. The general health of the people does not seem to have suffered. Indeed, some Burmese doctors are coming to believe that dried buffalo blood can be as effective as that of the rhinoceros, both for heart complaints and as a general tonic. They argue that this is only to be expected, because of the similarity between the habitat and habits of the two animals.

Another encouraging development is the reduction in the use of horn and hide, and the increasing use of the urine of the rhinoceros as a medicine. The change began when the King of Nepal sent two Indian rhinoceroses to Rangoon Zoo as a gift in 1980. The urine, which is used as a treatment for chest ailments and colds, is given away free to those who come to collect it, bringing their own bottles.

These developments, brought about by financial problems rather than an artificial increase in the price of the products, show that in Burma at least there is some flexibility in the attitudes of doctors and their patients to traditional medicine. It is hardly likely that the *per capita* income of prosperous trading countries like Malaysia or Singapore will plummet in the same way, or that the price of rhinoceros products will rise beyond the reach of the wealthiest people. However, if the flexibility is there, there is hope that in the next generation or two the use of genuine rhinoceros products might fall from favour. Again to take a Western parallel, the wearing of the skins of spotted and striped cats has become socially unacceptable in all but the crassest strata of the conspicuously rich.

The depressing side of Martin's report reveals that there is still a demand for certain rhinoceros products, so long as even a small supply is available. He met doctors who told him that although genuine dried rhinoceros blood was becoming hard to obtain, they were usually assured of a supply when they visited the hill states in the north. Hunters there still occasionally manage to find and kill rhinoceroses. When they do, they dry the blood and keep it until a doctor visits them, when they give it to him in exchange for his services. This indicates that the importance of the real thing has not dwindled where it can still be obtained. The pressure on the Sumatran rhinoceros in Burma will not decrease until the conservative tribesmen in the north can be convinced that its products no longer have any value. The onus of persuading them lies on the doctors who are the link between the hunters and the users of the blood.

Similarly depressing is the account of a medical hall in Mandalay, where horn, blood and hide were for sale to such customers as could still afford them. The only reason that hooves were not sold as well was that the doctors were unable to obtain them any more.

Japan, Korea, and the Future

Developments in Japan and Korea have been almost exactly opposite to those in Burma. A rising standard of living has gone hand in hand with a return to the traditional medical practices introduced from China over a thousand years ago. The significance of this is not to be underestimated: it shows the deeply held conviction among the Japanese in particular that Western medicine is dangerous for the patient. The danger is being recognised in the West as well, as long-term side effects become apparent, and the testing of drugs is repeatedly exposed as inadequate.

Although in the West the response is usually to develop new drugs with less pronounced side effects, there are many people who would rather turn to natural treatments because they are convinced that they are safer. A substantial industry exists to encourage them in their fears. There is a health food shop in every small town and suburb, catering for those who have lost their faith in synthetic medicines. The prices are usually higher than those for Western 'scientific' drugs, but since the patients who choose the treatments, in the West at least, are usually from the better-educated, and most often better-paid, levels of society, that does no harm to a very lucrative trade. It might not be long before health food shops start stocking medicines based on the Eastern tradition of horn and hide, as well as herbs and plant extracts.

At the time of Martin's surveys, the use of rhinoceros horn was very widespread in both Japan and Korea. Asian horn was preferred to the African variety, although it was expensive and hard to obtain. He found in 1981 that all imports of horn had officially been stopped in September 1980, but that from January to August of that year 763 kilos were imported, nearly all of African origin. This was clearly to beat the ban imposed by Japan's ratification of CITES in November 1980.

No other rhinoceros products are used in this school of medicine; but the horn, in sliced or ground form, is an ingredient of medicines to treat an astonishing range of diseases. Among them is the common cold: Martin asks what the Japanese are going to do about their colds when the present stocks run out. In the six years since his book was published, the official stocks must have been used up: the 1980 import, high though it was, was less than that for an average year during the 1970s. The evidence is that more 'Western' drugs are being used in Japan, not necessarily because they are thought to be more potent or effective, but because the supply of traditional drugs has ceased. If rhinoceros horn once more became legally available, it would no doubt find a ready market.

There is a move to develop substitutes for rhinoceros horn. Tests are being carried out, for example, on the horns of saiga antelope, a by-product of the commercial harvest of these animals for food in the USSR. Other medicines, which do not involve the use of horns, are also coming into the doctors' repertoire: dried worms are used at present for the treatment of fever, not as the best possible cure, but as an acceptable substitute.

The attack on the use of rhinoceros horn must be aimed very accurately if it is to have any effect. Traditional medicine is firmly entrenched in both Japan and Korea. The formal university training of doctors covers both Western pharmacology and traditional practices, side by side. The only hope is to convince the practitioners that they should find substitutes for rhinoceros horn in order to conserve the rhinoceros. Martin suggests the use of newspaper articles and stories for children as a useful first step: but if the effect of attempts to reduce the consumption of whale products in Japan is indicative of the public's response to this kind of propaganda, it is not likely to have much success. It might be more productive to provide funds to universities and medical schools for more experimental work on rhinoceros substitutes. A new generation of highly educated pharmacists emerging from the universities is the most likely vehicle for the transmission of new ideas as radical as this.

Despite the faith in traditional medicine, there is evidence that the demand for rhinoceros horn in Japan is decreasing, very largely as the result of CITES. The use of substitutes is being encouraged, not only by exporters of traditional medicines in Hong Kong, who want to fill the gap in their pharmacopoeia, and therefore in their order books, but also by the Japanese government itself. Martin considers that two additional factors have added to the decline in the use of rhinoceros products: the abundance of fake rhinoceros horn which resulted from the sharp increase in price after CITES, and the fact that many people in Asian cities have heard of the decline in rhinoceros populations, and believe that there are now no more available. As he points out, neither of these factors is evidence that the typical customer for rhinoceros medicines appreciates the need for conservation.

There is some hope for the rhinoceros, as generations grow up in whose medication it has played no part, at first because it has become too scarce. Later, we might well hope, substitutes will have been discovered and accepted by the medical profession and by their patients in the countries which at present place such a pressure on the remaining stocks. One day the use of its horn might be regarded all over the world as an archaic curiosity, in the same way as a prescription for the treatment of fever by one Dr Watson, in England, in 1760. The patient was to swallow 'a spider gently bruised and wrapped in a raisin or spread upon bread and butter'.

10
Dagger Handles

In North Yemen, the most important badge of an adult Muslim man is the wearing of a ceremonial dagger, or *jambia*, in his belt. The leather belt itself, and the sheath which holds the dagger, are highly decorated, and full of social significance. If the decoration on the sheath is of strips of green-dyed sheepskin, and the dagger handle is made from the horn of a zebu bull, studded with brass reproductions of ancient Byzantine coins, the wearer is a man from the mountains. Wealthier men, and those with greater social standing, especially those from *Sayed* families, who claim descent from the Prophet, wear daggers whose sheaths are decorated with silver or gold filigree. In the 1950s the finest daggers were those with handles made from giraffe horn, carved and studded with silver.

The *jambia* is presented to a youth at his circumcision, when he reaches marriageable age, at twelve or fifteen years old. Thereafter, it is the symbol of his manhood, and of his dedication to the Muslim faith. It is used in ceremonial dances, brandished point downwards above the dancer's head. It also has a part to play in disputes before the sheikh, when each party in the argument gives his *jambia* to the sheikh to hold, as a symbol that he trusts the sheikh to defend his interests, and as a pledge that he will not take the law into his own hands, but abide by the sheikh's verdict. There are occasional outbreaks of violence, when the *jambia* is used as a weapon, but its principal function is symbolic and decorative. A smaller knife carried behind the *jambia* in the same sheath serves as an everyday tool, for domestic use.

When the wealth produced by the country's oil production rose to astronomic levels in the late 1960s and early 1970s, the standards of *jambia* fashion rose to new heights. Nowadays, the handles of the most expensive, and therefore the most prestigious, daggers are made from black rhinoceros horn.

The country of origin of the horn has changed over the years. Not so long ago, Yemeni daggers had handles carved from the horns of black rhinoceroses from Chad, Ethiopia or Somalia: the raw material was brought into Yemen by air from

Khartoum, along with a certain number of horns from Sudan. Between 1969 and 1977, 49,900 lb (22,645 kilos) of horn were imported, representing about 8,000 rhinoceroses killed. Between 1970 and 1986, as the trade continued, the world population of black rhinoceroses fell from 65,000 to 4,000.

The route by which the horn entered the country changed in 1983, when the government of Sudan took steps to prevent the export of rhinoceros horn from their country, after they had become a member of CITES. The source of the materials changed for the simple reason that the black rhinoceros had become scarce or extinct in the countries from which the horn had previously been taken. More recently, it has been imported from Djibouti, either by air, or by dhow across the narrows of the Red Sea. The rhinoceroses have been dying further south, in the Central African Republic, East Africa and Zambia.

The latest population surveys from these countries suggest that there, too, the black rhinoceros population has fallen so low that hunting is no longer worth the effort. Now, the hunting has spread to the southern border of Zambia and across the Zambesi into Zimbabwe. Rumours are reaching Britain suggesting that the black rhinoceros population of the Luangwa Valley has been shot out, causing the poachers to range across the river. Counter-rumours, it must be said, report that the terrain in many parts of Luangwa is too rugged for any hunting to succeed in wiping out the rhinoceros. There are those who say that possibly hundreds of rhinoceroses are safe there. Whatever the truth might turn out to be, the poachers are turning their attention to Zimbabwe's much better-guarded rhinoceroses, and risking their lives in order to get horns to take back to their paymasters.

A single horn is worth more than a year's wages to a poacher. A haul of 32 horns confiscated by wardens at Kariba National Park in 1986 was valued at $1.6 million, or $50,000 each, on the open market. Probably less than one per cent of that sum goes to the poacher, but it still represents a substantial fortune to a rural African. To earn so much money in one hunting expedition is plainly enough to tempt men to risk their lives: in the first three months of 1987 at least 23 poachers who had crossed the river from Zambia were shot dead on Zimbabwe's northern border. The value of the horn to the middlemen who pay, equip and organise the poachers is only a fraction of its value as a finished article. It is said that a well-finished dagger can be sold in North Yemen for over $20,000, to a wealthy *Sayed*, often to present to his son.

The profitability of the trade does not stop when the horn has reached the carver. Most of the artists who make the finest *jambias* live and work in the capital, Sanaa. They are able to sell their shavings to merchants who re-export them to eastern Asia, where they are sold for medicinal use. Until very recently, this was perfectly legal under Yemeni law.

Dr Esmond Bradley Martin visited North Yemen in 1985, continuing his survey of the uses of rhinoceros horn around the world. His report, in *Oryx* in October of that year, summarised the trade in horn for dagger handles as it then existed. He pointed out that although importing rhinoceros horn to North Yemen became illegal in August 1982, the law was not enforced. The result of the ban was simply to increase by a factor of eight the bribe necessary to clear the horn through customs. This, he says, is evidence that the authorities are 'putting some pressure on the importers'.

The pressure has been on for other reasons, too. An economic slump which began in 1985 caused the government to seek ways of increasing revenue, and one method which they put into force at once was to tighten up the controls on smuggling. Furthermore, the government had become sensitive to the criticism from conservation bodies, and especially from the world's press, of the effect which North Yemen alone had been having on the black rhinoceros population. The average annual import of horn fell from 3,750 lb (1,700 kg) between 1980 and 1984, to less than 2,200 lb (1,000 kg) in 1985, and only 1,100 lb (500 kg) in 1986.

Dr Martin had already advocated the use of propaganda, in the form of radio and television programmes, as a way of persuading the dagger-buying public not to support the trade in rhinoceros horn: he pointed out that all the people who could afford to buy the most expensive daggers now have television sets and radios. He also suggested that daggers with zebu (cattle) or water buffalo horn handles could be made more attractive to the buyers by using better quality blades, and adding more expensive decoration. Other conservationists have suggested that it would be more to the point to start marketing daggers with solid silver or gold handles, to keep the price up among the most conspicuously expensive luxuries. However, at the present time the fall in oil revenues may make cheaper daggers more attractive.

An important point which Dr Martin makes is that very few *jambias* are made with rhinoceros horn handles: they are destined to be worn only by the very wealthiest members of society. Because of this, preventing any import of rhinoceros horn into North Yemen would not put dagger-makers out of business. Every Yemeni male must have his *jambia*; and the vast majority of them are made relatively simply, from cheap materials. Nevertheless, half the rhinoceros horn sold annually in the world ends up in North Yemen, in a dagger-maker's workshop in Sanaa. Clearly, if the trade could be stopped, by diplomatic or other means, the plight of the black rhinoceros would be significantly improved.

Such an improvement came about on 31 December 1986, when a cabinet meeting of the government of North Yemen decided to implement a six-point strategy to stop the trade in rhinoceros horn. The strategy had been worked out earlier that month at a meeting between Dr Martin, Lucy Vigne, a prominent conservationist working for rhinoceroses, and the Yemeni ministers of foreign affairs and the economy. The six points, as published in *BBC Wildlife* magazine in June 1987, were as follows:

—a personal approach by the Prime Minister to the single trader who had been responsible for two-thirds of all the imports, to warn him to stop handling new supplies;
—discussions between the foreign minister and a senior official of the United Arab Emirates, about the need to close down the trade routes for rhinoceros horn where they passed through his country;
—the prohibition of all rhinoceros horn exports from North Yemen, to stop the trade in shavings from the carvers' workshops;
—a pronouncement by the grand mufti, the senior religious figure in the country, that to cause the extinction of an animal species is against the will of God;
—an 'affidavit system', in which each dagger-maker would be required to agree not to use any more rhinoceros horn after the issue of his next licence, on pain of

having his shop closed if he broke his word;
—the elimination of import duties on water-buffalo horn, to make it an attractive substitute for rhinoceros horn.

By March 1987, the first three of these points had been put into practice, and the affidavit system was to be in effect by the end of the year. Because the manufacture of *jambias* is almost completely restricted to one area of the city of Sanaa, the authorities should find it relatively easy to police, and there is suddenly every reason to hope that the trade in rhinoceros horn dagger handles may be coming to an end. The benefits will stretch far south into Africa, possibly bringing an end to the bush war between poachers and Park guardians which has cost so much money and so many lives in the last few years.

11
Field Conservation in Africa

The three principal enemies of rhinoceroses in Africa are human hunters, drought and shortage of habitat. Predation by other animals hardly troubles them, though young rhinoceroses are sometimes taken by hyaenas. The conservation of rhinoceroses in their present dangerous plight must involve protecting them from all their enemies, in proportion to the threat posed by each.

Protection from poachers has become the most important factor in the conservation of the black rhinoceros, because of the enormous value of their horns. In 1982, the rhinoceros population of the Central African Republic was estimated at 3,000 animals: today, it is at the point of extinction. Poachers have reduced the population of the Masai Mara in Kenya by 90 per cent in the last ten years. In 1970, the black rhinoceros population of Kenya was between 18,000 and 20,000; by 1986, it was below 500. In recent years, especially in northern Zimbabwe, the game parks have become a battleground, with mounting casualties as the poachers, armed with ever more powerful weapons, take bigger and bigger risks. A large proportion of the funds for rhinoceros conservation is being spent on survey aircraft, radio equipment and weapons, to combat the influx of poachers into protected areas.

Opinions differ about the morality of killing people to protect an animal species, no matter how endangered. Between 1984 and 1986, game wardens in Zimbabwe killed 27 poachers; and in the first three months of 1987, they are said to have killed 23 more. It is a full-scale war, with complicated logistics and a sophisticated intelligence system on both sides. In the same period, at least 200 black rhinoceroses were killed in Kariba National Park.

There are some conservationists who find it difficult to support such a blood-thirsty operation, though without the efforts of the 70 armed guards who patrol 150 miles (240 km) of river bank separating the Park from Zambia there would undoubtedly be many fewer surviving rhinoceroses, if any at all. As a holding operation, in the form of an orderly retreat, Prime Minister Robert Mugabe has personally authorised a grant to finance the removal of rhinoceroses from the front line: 110 had been moved by June 1987. The armed guards were still in full military action, however, holding off the marauding poachers while the retreat went on.

Whatever one's views, the out-and-out bush war which has developed between poachers and wardens is plainly not a long-term strategy for the conservation of the black rhinoceros, or any other animal. Where one group of people is occupied in killing another, new emotions creep into the conflict, so that it is possible to imagine that one day, even when the trade in rhinoceros horn has stopped and the animals are of no value to the poachers, the war will go on, for reasons of revenge, pride, or simply bravado.

The Nature of the Poacher

A poacher is defined as a hunter who kills game on land which does not belong to him, in defiance of the law. In Britain, not long ago, the poacher was a folk hero, admired rather than despised by the common people. His clandestine activities, and the brutality of the punishments which were inflicted on him when he was caught, won him the sympathy of his neighbours — except those in the Big House, who owned the land. Traditional songs such as 'The Gallant Poacher' express the feelings of the people for the victim, and for the gamekeeper.

> The bravest shot amongst our lot,
> 'twas his misfortune to be shot:
> but his deeds will ne'er be forgot
> by those he left below.
> The murd'ring hand that did him kill,
> and on the ground his blood did spill
> shall wander e'er against his will,
> and find no resting place.

The reason for this apparent condonement of crime by otherwise law-abiding citizens was that the laws were widely perceived to be unjust. How, it was asked, can anyone claim to own a rabbit or a hare? They are wild animals which live where they please, without help or hindrance from the man who happens to hold the deeds to a particular piece of ground. The answer lay far back in history, when rabbits in particular were nurtured and protected by the landowner as a valuable food source, soon after they were first introduced into Britain. The laws persisted long after rabbits became so numerous as to be declared a pest. Later, as agriculture spread, animals such as hares and deer were protected by landowners from foxes and poachers alike, for sport as well as food.

The old attitude of the poacher and his supporters persisted, however: it was, and is, based on the feeling that the land and its wild produce belong to everyone. Some farmers and landowners feel the same, and allow the hunting of rabbits and hares across their land. This cuts little ice with the poacher. Indeed, there are some poachers today, one of whom is an old friend of mine in the county of Gloucestershire, who will only hunt on land where such permission has been explicitly denied. With them, poaching is as much a sport, or even a political act, as it is a means of filling the pot.

In Africa, a similar situation arose when, as Ron Thomson says in his *On Wildlife*

'*Conservation*', 'the white man perceived an increase in the illegal marketing of elephant ivory and rhinoceros horn (and) recommended to the black governments of Africa that they impose bans on the hunting of these species'. In fact, as Thomson says elsewhere, the problem arose before the black market in rhinoceros horn and other products became anything like as lucrative as it is now, when the game laws which were put into force were intended principally to protect the white man's sport. Their chief effect was that rural tribesmen could not legally hunt any more on land which had been their larder for generations. The hunters whose activities were essential for the survival of their villages were branded 'poachers', and regarded by the authorities as criminals. In just the same way as in Britain, poaching became a dangerous necessity, and the poacher an admired figure in village society.

That attitude persists today in many rural parts of Africa. In the past, animals which were not killed for food may have had to be killed because they were encroaching on the land needed for agriculture, or because they were attacking stock, or even people. The man who killed them gained the gratitude of his neighbours, all the more so if he did it at the risk of his liberty. Increasing the anti-poaching patrols in National Parks has prevented the killing of game near to the beaten track, but in places where there is little chance of anyone hearing a rifle shot, hunting continues whenever the chance arises. Increasing the patrols still further only stimulates the hunters to rise to the added challenge: the thing becomes a game, albeit rather a dangerous one. The fate of Gladys and Gertie at Amboseli, speared by the Masai as an act of bravado, is a good illustration of this. It is parallel in its defiance to the attitude of my friend the Gloucestershire poacher.

Without wishing in the slightest to condone the act, this is the background against which one might consider the rise of the modern kind of poaching, in which heavily-armed men slaughter rhinoceroses to take their horns for financial gain. The market which they are supplying is so insatiable, and the rewards so great, that they are evidently prepared to risk their lives in a war against the government. However, they also hold an honoured position among their fellows which derives from an earlier era of poaching.

It is almost impossible to imagine the rural Africans over whose land these raids take place being in a position to do anything about it — even, as Ron Thomson would add, if they wanted to. He makes the point most strongly that every new Land Rover and every new radio-equipped game ranger reinforces the mistrust and hatred which the rural African feels for those who try to enforce the game laws. Even if they were 100 per cent on the side of the Western campaigners against poaching, they would be powerless against weaponry of the kind which is used by the poachers. However, they are not even one per cent on the Western side: on the contrary, they benefit to a small extent from assisting the activities of the poachers, receiving gifts of money and meat for their services.

The conclusion of this argument is inescapable: reinforcing the game rangers will not stop the poachers. Even 'educating' rural Africans into sharing the white man's attitude to wildlife cannot be a lasting answer. The answer must come from Africa, and be acceptable to Africans on their own terms. The wildlife which surrounds them must somehow be made valuable to them, so that they will cultivate and protect it for reasons which make practical sense. Thomson's book proposes a way in which this can be encouraged, based on sound wildlife management.

Wildlife Management

The ecological basis for wildlife management has been established for a long time: it begins with the concept of *carrying capacity*. The carrying capacity dictates how many animals can live in a particular place. For any species of animal, it is defined by the food supply, the water supply and the space available. For the African rhinoceroses, the requirements of each species are known well enough for the carrying capacity of any area to be determined. Field conservation of rhinoceroses may involve manipulating the carrying capacity of an area for their benefit, not necessarily to the detriment of the other species of animal which live there.

For example, the requirement of black rhinoceroses to remain within 3 miles (5 km) of water gives an opportunity to a wildlife manager to increase the carrying capacity of his terrain by providing waterholes the correct distance apart. The different food requirements of black and white rhinoceroses permit manipulation of the habitat in favour of one or other species. Study of the territorial needs of males and females at various times of the year will reveal another aspect of the carrying capacity.

The rhinoceroses as a group are hardly troubled by predation when they are adult; but young black rhinoceros calves are vulnerable to the attentions of spotted hyaenas, and in some areas such predation is a significant factor in limiting the expansion of the rhinoceros population. The organised removal of spotted hyaenas is, therefore, an essential part of manipulating the habitat in favour of black rhinoceroses.

All of these factors must be considered when the aim is to preserve the population in an emergency. At a later stage, manipulation may be gradually reduced, until the populations of all the animals in the park find an equilibrium: but it would be a rare park which could survive in such a state for long without active human intervention.

Heroic Intervention

In his remarkable if somewhat polemical book, Ron Thomson, Director of Bophuthatswana National Parks and Wildlife Management Board, describes a course of action which he believes will restore the fortunes of the black rhinoceros to the level of the white, which was so successfully brought back from the brink of extinction in Natal during the 1960s.

The attitude of the book is well expressed in its title, where the buzz-word 'Conservation' is in inverted commas. Thomson's experience in the field, principally in Zimbabwe, makes him uniquely qualified to comment on the effect on the public of the well-intended conservation efforts of international bodies such as the World Wildlife Fund. Since his methods often involve heroic manipulation of the environment and the animals, using 'heroic' in the surgical sense of 'drastic', he has been well-placed to appreciate the horrified protests of the uninformed.

Thomson's work with the elephants of Hwange National Park drew consider-

Plate 14: Indian rhinos divide their home range into 'public' and 'private' areas. 'Private' paths such as this one are defended by their owners against other individuals.

Plate 15: Indian rhinoceroses can mate for over an hour: it has been suggested that this is one reason for the belief in the aphrodisiac powers of rhinoceros horn.

able criticism because it involved shooting whole family groups at once: the critics seemed unable to understand that it was done in this way for the benefit of the elephants themselves, to maintain the population of the Park in a healthy condition. There comes a point at which no more elephants can be transported to zoos or to other locations, and at that point, to put it unsentimentally, some of the population must die. The social organisation of elephants makes it preferable for their future management that they should be killed in complete family groups, with some very young animals being removed for relocation in other protected areas, or occasionally zoos. The uproar from what Ron Thomson would call 'conserva-tionists' (complete with inverted commas) can easily be imagined.

Part of the controversy centred around Thomson's argument that if the ivory and skins from the culled elephants were to be marketed properly, the whole operation would make a profit for the Park. For suggesting this, he came in for renewed criticism from all sides of the 'conservation' lobby. His suggestions for the restoration of the black rhinoceros population led to a no less controversial conclusion.

Drawing on a considerable body of research as well as on his own experience, Thomson has determined that rhinoceros populations increase most quickly when they are at between 50 and 60 per cent of the carrying capacity of their habitat. The course from this point is clear: if the aim is to increase the population of black rhinoceroses, the population and the carrying capacity must be manipulated until the one is half of the other.

As the population increases beyond the optimum figure, some of the surplus animals must be relocated into areas where their numbers are as near as possible half the carrying capacity. Carrying out such a plan demands a considerable amount of skill in moving rhinoceroses around. The techniques are established by now, not least by Thomson himself, following his work with the white rhinoceros. Terrain to receive new populations of black rhinoceroses must be selected from a precise knowledge of their optimum habitat, and prepared to receive them, for example by the provision of waterholes and the removal of spotted hyaenas.

Ultimately, when all available habitats were occupied, or when the managers had decided that the population was at a viable level in a sufficient number of places, excess individuals would become the legitimate quarry of sport hunters. Because of its rarity, whether or not it had any commercial value once it had been shot, the black rhinoceros would be sought after by the very wealthiest hunters in the world. This policy has worked for other species in Zimbabwe, in Uganda (in the past), and in South Africa, with the white rhinoceros in particular. In Pilanesberg National Park, ten mature white rhinoceros bulls are shot each year as trophies, earning the Park $10,000 each. Ron Thomson estimates that because of its rarity a black rhinoceros would be worth at least $25,000. He calls it 'the most valuable trophy in Africa today'.

By the time it had reached the stage at which it could be hunted in a sustainable way, a stable black rhinoceros population would at the very least finance the protected areas where it lived and the staff needed to maintain them, and at best would be earning valuable foreign exchange for its homeland, as part of a self-financing wildlife resource.

However, as soon as the exploitation stage was reached, massive controversy would arise, powered by what Thomson terms the 'irrationalities' implanted in people's minds by the failure of communication between the conservation organisations and the public. This is not entirely fair; but one of the attractions of reading Thomson, or indeed talking to him, is that he is a dedicated and witty man, and never entirely fair. Not least among the problems will be the fact that the conservation bodies have spent years, and millions, telling the world that the black rhinoceros is an endangered species. It might well take them years and millions more to convince the world that the endangered species may now be shot for sport.

At this point, it would probably be as well to postpone discussion of what we are to do with a restored black rhinoceros population until we have one firmly established in at least one country.

We have plenty of time for the discussion. Years of research will be needed to evaluate the carrying capacity and rhinoceros populations even of the restricted areas where they now live. It will take a great deal of money to carry out the operation, and it will be a long time before it starts to finance itself. If these two needs could be fulfilled, there is no reason why Thomson's plan should not succeed as magnificently as the Natal Parks Board's Operation Rhino, which brought the white rhinoceros out of reach of danger and, indeed, into the realm of remunerative licensed hunting by wealthy foreigners.

Thomson states categorically that the populations of black rhinoceros in the Zululand game reserves are the only available source from which his plan could be carried out: populations elsewhere in Africa are too thin on the ground. However, at least one Zululand population, that of Hluhluwe Game Reserve, shows signs of stress. The animals are said to be in poor condition, maturing at a later age than black rhinoceroses elsewhere, and with a longer interval between calves. This is not because they are overcrowded on the ground, but because of a near-disaster to the Hluhluwe population which occurred between 1961 and 1985. What happened during that period is a very good example of the effect of changing the carrying capacity of a habitat.

In 1961, the population was about 300 animals; by 1971 there were 199; and in 1985 the numbers had fallen to below 100. The reason for the decline, according to Peter Hitchins, quoted in Thomson's book, was to be found in the events of 1954 to 1972. During this period, 33,115 large herbivores were removed from the Park, including wildebeeste, zebra, warthog, impala and nyala. Once they were gone, the grass grew up tall and thick, with nothing to eat it. The result was an outbreak of fires, which reduced the large, dense acacia thickets where the black rhinoceroses used to feed. Short of food, the population crashed, until it had reached the new carrying capacity of the area. The population is still as large as it can be, but it is one-third of what it was before because of the reduction in carrying capacity of the Park.

Paradoxically, this is good news: it seems that we already have a donor population for the first transplant operation, as soon as a suitable area of recipient habitat has been located. The operation will probably not go unopposed: Thomson relates the outcry which arose when five black rhinoceroses were donated to an American organisation from Zululand. He blames the fuss on 'the persistent propaganda of wildlife administrations and the media', which had stressed the endangered species status of the black rhinoceros, but touched lightly if at all on the fact that the five exported animals represented less than two per cent of the overall population of the province. Their removal, he says, had no impact at all on the population of the species in Zululand.

Three other populations look as if they are at or near their carrying capacity, and Thomson calculates that there could be as many as 100 black rhinoceroses available in Zululand now for relocation when required.

To judge the likely success of the operation, he reviews the fate of 46 black rhinoceroses released into Hwange (then called Wankie) National Park in Zimbabwe (then called Rhodesia), in 1963–5. Since only 18 were female, he bases his calculations on an effective release of 36 animals (18 breeding pairs). In only 20 years the population had more than doubled, to 80. Conditions were less than ideal, since although the terrain was very suitable, spotted hyaena were very numerous: but the animals succeeded all the same.

In Addo Elephant National Park, the success was spectacular, the population rising from two pairs to 19 individuals in 23 years. In addition to the 19 survivors, nine had died and three had been removed to protected areas elsewhere. Thomson calculates this as an effective increase of 22 animals, on the grounds that some of the nine died avoidably from errors in management, and that natural mortality during the period ought to have been about five.

If the Addo population can increase from four to 26 (nearly 600 per cent) in 23 years, he concludes, the total number of black rhinoceros in Africa south of the Limpopo and Cunene Rivers could rise from 600 to over 3,000 in the next two decades. Then we could begin the debate about what to do with it.

Save the Rhino, Rhino Rescue and Others

The Save the Rhino Trust, which has been in operation in Zambia since 1980, working for elephants as well as rhinoceroses, received a huge boost in 1984 and 1985, when it was given major donations from NORAD, the Norwegian Agency for International Development. It is also supported by the World Wildlife Fund, as well as by the Zambian Department of National Parks and Wildlife Service. Part of the money has been used to build a Safari Lodge in the Luangwa Valley, a project which is not as extravagant as it might seem at first glance. The Lodge is a capital and a diplomatic investment. It not only attracts tourists, whose money provides funding for the anti-poaching work; it also shows the problems of poaching to potentially influential foreigners at first hand, creating international awareness which must stand the government in good stead as it continues its efforts to protect the country's dwindling wildlife.

Another agency has already begun work in Kenya, to start the first phase of a relocation and re-establishment scheme, in the wake of the disastrous reduction in black rhinoceros numbers there since 1970. The Rhino Rescue Trust is building a sanctuary in Lake Nakuru National Park, into which 20 black rhinoceroses will be relocated from small populations elsewhere in the country. The sanctuary will be protected by armed guards, and surrounded by an electric fence of a kind which has already proved its effectiveness in restraining rhinoceroses elsewhere. A good deal of money will be needed for the work, and the effort to raise it has already begun.

▼▼

The publicity machine rolled into action early in 1987, when a series of newspaper articles appeared in the British press. One, in the *Observer* newspaper's colour supplement, described a series of flights in an ultra-light aircraft over the Masai Mara by a couple of Frenchmen. Amongst four double-page photographs of the flight, the text gave an account of the difficulties and dangers of the operation, with only a brief summary of the aims of the Rhino Rescue Trust. An article in the *Daily Telegraph* a week later did not mention the flight, but gave a similar account of Rhino Rescue. An important difference was that the latter article gave figures for the cost of the operation, and appealed for funds, with addresses in the UK and Kenya to which donations could be sent. (The addresses can be found at the back of this book.) The sanctuary will cost a total of £420,000, with an additional £2,000 needed for each of the 20 rhinoceroses, for darting and relocation.

The *Telegraph* article contained a number of inaccuracies. For example, it reinforced the myth that 'it is believed in the East that a powder made from the creature's horn is a powerful aphrodisiac'. It also described an attack made 'at the first whiff or sound of danger' by 'an irascible, unpredictable, dangerous 3000 lbs of charging armour'. One gnashes one's teeth at such misrepresentation, but the gnashing might be misplaced. The errors may well be irrelevant in this context. The point and purpose of articles such as these is to tap charitable resources for the benefit of the species, almost regardless of which species it is. Ron Thomson might decry such articles as emotional and irrational; but from another point of view, if they bring in the money, they are achieving their end.

There is no reason why the information used in these fund-raising efforts should not be accurate, however. Indeed, people might be even more willing to give money if they knew the size of the medicinal trade in rhinoceros products, for example, or that the horns are used for the handles not of 'hunting knives', as the *Telegraph* writer called them, but of an essential item of masculine status in the 'Arabian States' to which he referred. Whether accurate information draws more substantial contributions to the cause will no doubt become apparent shortly, when a few people have read this book. . .

One Man's Campaign

Michael Werikhe, a young Kenyan wildlife enthusiast, has begun a personal campaign for rhinoceros conservation. In 1982 and 1985 he undertook long sponsored walks, the first from his home town of Mombasa to Nairobi, and the second from Kampala, across Kenya to Dar-es-Salaam, and back to Mombasa. The walks have received very little coverage in the European or American press so far, though in Kenya they have not gone unnoticed. An international campaign, with walks in Europe and the United States, is planned for 1988, with much greater publicity designed to attract funds from all over both countries. All the funds which Werikhe's campaign raises are destined for the rhinoceros translocation work in his home country, though the present position being what it is some of the money will have to be spent on radios and rifles.

There are many schemes like this, supporting one or other of the established rhinoceros appeals. They have a lot in common with other long-running appeals, for the tiger and the panda for example, in that many of the contributors will never

▲▲

have seen the subject of the rescue operation in its natural habitat. They are much more likely to have been influenced by seeing the species on television, perhaps inspired by a programme to plan, or at least to dream about, a safari holiday in China, India or Africa. Whatever their motivation, the money which comes in from such international appeals is the only hope at present for the effective conservation of endangered species world-wide.

Although they supply the trained staff and the local expertise to carry out the conservation operations in the field, it would be unreasonable to expect African governments to make any major financial contributions to the work; they have other priorities for the disposal of such large sums of money as are needed. Because of this, though, there is a real danger that the conservation of rhinoceroses will be seen to be financed principally by non-Africans, apparently for the benefit of foreign tourists. As usual, it will be argued that tourism is an important contributor to the national economies, but this cuts little ice with the rural Africans who are in the front line of the war with the poachers.

Advertisers and Propaganda

The conservation of the black rhinoceros is a vital undertaking, and it might well be argued that it is immaterial whether funds for the work come from the home governments or from outside Africa. Many of the scientists involved in the research, and all the game rangers who defend the reserves, sometimes at the risk of their own lives, are Africans. The governments of the countries in which the work is done, even if they cannot make substantial financial contributions, give their support in other ways.

The missing ingredient is the involvement of ordinary African people. To them, a rhinoceros is neither a mystical beast, nor a living fossil to be preserved for its curiosity value, still less the symbol of a wonderful holiday. To an African villager, it is either an agricultural nuisance or an occasional source of funds in the form of donations from poachers. There is at present no great feeling that 'we Kenyans' can gain from conserving the black rhinoceros. Instead, a group of urban Kenyans, who seem to the rural majority amongst whom they work to constitute an alien 'they', are seen as the prime movers in an operation whose main beneficiaries will be tourists from overseas. Somehow, the villagers must be brought into the action, by being made aware of the benefits to them of a stable, exploitable rhinoceros population in 20 or 30 years' time.

Michael Werikhe's work, talking to young people as he walked from village to village, has undoubtedly converted many of those who met him to a new way of thinking about the rhinoceroses around them, few though they are. It is unlikely that he was able to convince them of any immediate and tangible benefit from preserving the animals, however, and there lies the major problem in the conservation of the black rhinoceros in particular, and rhinoceroses in general. The answer will have to come from expert communicators who can plan and carry out a long-term propaganda operation aimed at changing people's attitudes. In short, the advertising industry.

For advertisers to plan a campaign, they need to know the desired result. The debate at the field end of the conservation effort will not be settled until the rural

Africans recognise that the protection of wildlife in general, and rhinoceroses in particular, is in their own long-term interests. It may not be too soon to brief an advertising agency, to start spreading the word by the best means possible. One thing is clear, however: protecting African rhinoceroses with guns and electric fences paid for by money from outside the country and organised from the cities can only be a short-term holding operation.

12

Conservation in Asia

The threats to the Asian rhinoceros are different from those in Africa. Poaching is less organised, probably because there are not enough surviving animals to make it worthwhile. It still occurs, but incidents are rare enough to be reported individually as they happen, not clumped together as part of a general scene as they are in southern Africa. In Nepal, which is worth considering in detail, poaching is very rare indeed but other human pressures pose a serious problem. The way in which this is being approached suggests a solution to similar conflicts of interest in other parts of the world.

People and Parks in Nepal

Nepal is a stable monarchy, in which an all-powerful King makes it his personal concern to protect rhinoceroses, which have an important place in the history and traditions of the country. This was not always the case: during the 1950s, when Nepal was in a state of political turmoil, there was considerable carnage among the rhinoceroses of the swampy grasslands of the terai, especially in Chitwan, which was then the royal hunting preserve. Chitwan became a National Park in 1973, to protect the rhinoceroses and tigers which survived there. From the start, the rules were very firmly enforced by the new King. Detachments of the Royal Nepalese Army patrol the park twice daily, supported outside its borders by the Rhinoceros Patrol of the Royal Nepalese Forest Department. Poaching is almost completely unheard of: but because certain parts of the rhinoceros are important to the people for ritual or medicinal reasons, as I have described in Chapter 6, any rhinoceros which dies in the Park is made available to them, principally as a source of hide. This makes poaching even less likely, since admittedly small but adequate pieces of hide may be bought for important rituals at perfectly reasonable prices. No doubt the regular patrols by armed and trained soldiers are an added deterrent.

The principal problem in Nepal is the indirect threat to the rhinoceros population which comes from the intense human population pressure on the boundaries of national parks and other reserves. A recent study among the villagers who live around the borders of Chitwan illustrates the range of small factors which contribute to the difficulties of maintaining good relations between a National Park and the people who live nearby. It also shows evidence of a humane and enlightened attitude in Nepal to the interactions between Parks and people. The involvement of ordinary people is an important part of Nepalese government, down to the smallest political unit, called a *panchayat*, consisting of five elders whose responsibilities make them the close equivalent of a village or parish council.

The study was carried out in 1986 by Mr Uday Raj Sharma, the Chief Warden of Royal Chitwan National Park, with a grant from the US Appeal of the World Wildlife Fund. His objective was to look at the conflict of interests 'from the people's side of the fence'.

He found that there were two principal areas of conflict: damage to crops by herbivores, including rhinoceroses, emerging from the Park at night, and the shortage of firewood and grass outside the Park, which tempted villagers to invade the protected area in search of supplies. There have also been instances of cattle, and even people, being attacked by tigers from the Park, but these are very rare. The most recent was in December 1985, when three people and ten cattle were killed by one marauding tiger, which was subsequently shot.

There are 37 separate *panchayats* bordering on Royal Chitwan National Park. They differ in their individual circumstances, but the overall picture is similar in them all: a dense population, growing at about 2.6 per cent per year, supplemented by large numbers of illegal squatters. All these people have to find fuel for themselves and fodder for their cattle from a rapidly deteriorating remainder of forest outside the Park. Park guards regularly round up invading cattle, which may have strayed but are more likely to have been driven into the Park. The cattle should be impounded, but for lack of water within the Park, they are usually simply driven out again. Arrests for stealing firewood and grass from the Park are common: there were 550 prosecutions in the year 1985–6.

These incursions into the Park have a damaging effect on the animals, especially rhinoceroses, which the Park was set up to protect. The animals themselves, not only rhinoceroses but chital deer, wild boar and flocks of parakeets, have an equally deleterious effect on the crops of the people who live nearby. The damage is worse where there is no obvious natural boundary dividing the Park from the agricultural land, such as a river or a ridge of higher ground.

After exhaustive enquiries, Sharma formed a picture of a basically law-abiding population, driven by shortages to break the law of the land. Some admitted freely that stealing from the Park was their only way of getting firewood. Others were not feeling the pinch to quite the same extent, because they live in the areas of forest outside the Park which, in spite of heavy felling during the 1950s, still provide sufficient fodder and fuel. However, it was plain that overgrazing of these areas, and lopping the crowns of the trees to feed cattle, would soon put these fortunate *panchayats* into the same state of shortage as their neighbours.

The solutions which Sharma proposes in his report fall into two categories, for the short and the long term. To ease the firewood problem in the short term, he suggests that Park staff should collect dead wood from within the Park, making depots from which villagers could collect it, perhaps for a nominal fee. Further, he remarks that although collecting driftwood from along the river banks is illegal, it is a common practice: he suggests that it should be legalised, but supervised. For the long term, he proposes the creation of managed forests, controlled by individual *panchayats*, which will provide fuel in a renewable cycle. For the first seven years or so, until the canopy closes, these new 'firewood forests' will even provide grazing for cattle among the trees.

Cattle are a great threat, in Nepal as they are elsewhere in subtropical climates, since unrestricted 'ranching', whether over village lands or inside the Park, can only lead to erosion, and will prevent the regeneration of the forest. Another serious danger is the transmission of diseases from the domestic herds to the wild ungulates in the Park.

Some *panchayats* already practise stall-feeding, bringing fodder to the beasts rather than letting them find their own. This has several advantages, one of which is that the dung can be collected and used to generate burnable gas, known in Nepal as 'gobar gas', thus easing the fuel shortage. Another advantage is that protecting areas of grass, which in some *panchayats* is cut for thatching material and sold to the villagers twice a year, also protects the river banks from erosion. 'Walking lanes' leading down to the river are used to take the cattle for a drink every day, but the rest of the land is used to grow grass which is cut and carried for fodder at regular intervals.

Since the *panchayats* are autonomous, there is a wide variety of approaches to the problems of fuel and fodder, but almost all of them tend to have the same result: the Park is being nibbled away around its edges. Pointing out that this has created an effective buffer zone between Park and people, Sharma regrets that the buffer zone is actually inside the Park. He proposes instead that a new buffer zone should be created, by managing existing forest remnants, and at the same time planting new ones, outside the Park, extending them outwards to natural boundaries such as the rivers and ridges which have shown their value in some places in keeping wildlife away from crops.

Sharma concludes his report with a plea to keep armed guards out of the buffer zone. If the people find the Park 'a nuisance', as some of them confessed they did, because it harbours animals which take their crops and occasionally their cattle, they find the daily presence of armed men an affront. Where the need for them is clear, they can be tolerated, for example in some of the patches of forest around the borders of the park which still survive in good condition. They could be exploited as hunting areas or for high-grade forestry management, and would need to be guarded against poachers and other intruders as closely as the Park itself: but the buffer zone should in the long run be free from weapons. As in Africa, where protecting wildlife at the point of a gun is at best a temporary solution, the best hope for the conservation of rhinoceroses in Nepal is to gain the willing co-operation of the people. The African rhinoceroses seem to be regarded as pests or profitable prey by the rural people: at least in Nepal they have a place in the country's traditional beliefs, so that they might be protected for their own sake.

The protection of rhinoceroses in Nepal has been a great success. The population of Royal Chitwan National Park is currently estimated at 400 individuals, with another 70 or so living outside the Park boundary. From 1974 to 1985, the net increase of the population was five animals per year. The time had clearly come to disperse the country's herd of one-horned rhinoceroses, to protect it in case of any disaster which might overtake the grasslands and forest which are at present its only home.

In a natural forest, fire may be a regular feature of the ecology, with a longer or shorter period of regeneration to follow before the habitat is restored to its former state. Patches of forest which are burned out grow back quite quickly, because they are surrounded by the right species of trees, producing seedlings which compete to fill the gap as soon as possible. The animals which live in such continuous forest have somewhere else to go, so that a fire is only a minor inconvenience. Where the forest is limited in extent, by being surrounded by cultivated land in this case, a serious fire could make all its animal inhabitants homeless, with nowhere else to go for the decades which might be needed for the old forest to grow up again. This is why fire precautions are so vital, of course, but all wildlife managers know that it is impossible to guard against every eventuality. Thus the chance to move some of the most precious animals to another site is one to be seized with both hands.

Seizing a rhinoceros is not a matter to be undertaken lightly, as we shall see in the next section; but early in 1986, four animals were captured outside the boundary of Royal Chitwan National Park, using tranquilliser darts, and transported by road to the Royal Bardia Wildlife Reserve, in western Nepal. Bardia was a known haunt of rhinoceroses until 1900, when they were finally hunted out. The United States Air Force offered to provide an airlift, but the offer was refused with thanks: 16 hours on the road were thought to be less traumatic than being loaded in and out of an Air Force transport. The journey was accomplished successfully, without harm to the animals.

The three females and one male were found to be in good health one month after their arrival. A year later, nine more animals were moved into the Reserve to join them, and all 13 will be closely watched to see whether they breed, and to make sure that they do not stray over the border of the Reserve into the agricultural land which reaches right up to its boundary. One method of preventing the animals from straying will be to set up a solar-powered electric fence along crucial parts of the Park boundary.

The operation was funded by the King Mahendra Trust for Nature Conservation, using grants from His Majesty's Government and from the World Wildlife Fund US Appeal, with transport and equipment provided by the Ministry of Public Works and the Timber Corporation. The total cost seems to have been about $12,000: a small enough sum to re-establish a new breeding nucleus of an endangered species in part of its former habitat.

Translocation in India

The problems of transporting rhinoceroses from place to place have been eased somewhat by the invention of immobilising drugs. When 'Operation Rhino' was carried out in Natal in 1961, drugs were used, although they were in their infancy. At the time, many wildlife managers thought it was safer to capture the animals in the old way, by lassoing them from a Land Rover, an adventurous proceeding to say the least. There were no casualties from the use of drugs in Operation Rhino, but that was put down by some people to luck, though others claimed staunchly that everything was under control. Whatever the truth of the matter, the Natal

Parks Board were working with a large and stable population of upwards of 1,500 animals. When the time came to divide the rhinoceros population in Assam, the managers were dealing with the last sizeable population of an endangered species in the country, and they had to exercise great care not to harm it.

The population in Kaziranga National Park numbers over a thousand animals, however, and it was considered safe enough to try to relocate some of them to another protected place.

The problems for the rhinoceros in Assam are the familiar trio of poaching, loss of habitat and the risk of disease. Although the poaching is not organised to the same degree as it is in Africa, it is heavy, supplying the lucrative Far Eastern medical market, where Asian horn has always commanded a far higher price than that from Africa. The loss of habitat is another example of a long chain of events ending in damage to the environment and its wildlife. It is the result of erosion, which is caused by flooding, which in its turn is the product of extensive deforestation in the catchment areas around the Park, because there are too many people trying to live there.

Disease is a particular threat in Assam, not only because the rhinoceros population is very densely crowded in Kaziranga, but because there are still some rhinoceroses outside the park which occasionally mingle with domestic cattle. Any cattle sickness which came into the rhinoceros herd from neighbouring domestic stock might quickly reach epidemic proportions. It was time to break up the herd.

In 1981, a committee under the chairmanship of Dr John B. Sale, Chief Technical Adviser to the FAO in India, recommended a suitable site for a trial translocation. After two years of field work, complete with botanical surveys, they had selected part of Dudhwa National Park, in the swampy grassland of the terai in Uttar Pradesh. Rhinoceroses had lived there within the last century, so the committee was fulfilling the requirement of the Species Survival Commission's Asian Rhino Specialist Group that the establishment of additional breeding groups should be within the former distribution range of the species. The new site was protected from poaching within a well-managed park, it offered good habitat with a plentiful food and water supply, and it was well out of range of the nearest herds of domestic cattle.

The area of the Park which was chosen consisted of 35 sq miles (90 sq km) of grassland. An independent botanical survey showed that it was capable of supporting approximately 90 rhinoceroses, and that it was not the only suitable area within the Park boundaries. There was room for expansion, once the new breeding herd became established. To make sure that the animals stayed within the best of the chosen area, and to prevent them from straying away into cultivated land nearby, an electric fence was set up to enclose 10 sq miles (27 sq km), the part of it nearest to cultivated land being strengthened by a rhinoceros-proof ditch to make doubly certain. Holding stockades were built inside this fenced area, to protect the rhinoceroses when they arrived.

While all these preparations were being made, Sale and his colleagues carried out tests with the drugs which they intended to use to immobilise the animals. The drugs had been used in Africa, but it was important to find out how the Indian rhinoceroses would react to them. Apart from the dangers of using the wrong dose, there were risks associated with immobilising a large, heavy animal for any protracted period. The tests established which dosages were safe, and gave an opportunity to practise the handling and transport techniques which would be needed when the time came.

The operation proper began early in 1984. A group of ten rhinoceroses was located outside Pobitara Sanctuary in Assam: they were highly vulnerable to poaching, and they had been invading cultivated land and damaging crops. They were plainly a good group to move. The vulnerability of the rhinoceroses was underlined when one of them was taken by poachers while the capture team was actually at work in the area.

If Thomson's principles were to be followed, the new area should have been stocked with half its carrying capacity, or 13 rhinoceroses, preferably all young adults: but Sale and his colleagues did not have the luxury of complete freedom of choice. In ten days they captured six out of the group of nine survivors, finishing with a rather motley collection, consisting of three females and three males. Two of the females were of advanced age — Sale calls them 'elderly' — and the other was subadult. The males included one large old specimen, one senior adult, and a young adult. They were put into a temporary stockade while they recovered from being captured. The large male escaped during the first night, but the others settled down to feed and wallow, seeming little the worse for their ordeal.

Nine days later, the remaining five animals were packed into crates, and driven to Guwahati Airport. From there they were flown to New Delhi in an aircraft chartered by the government, fed and watered, and driven to Dudhwa National Park to be unpacked into the holding stockades which had been prepared earlier. One of the elderly females died eleven days later, leaving four animals to be released into the Park after a holding period of three weeks. The older of the two males had been fitted with a radio collar, to make it easier to track his subsequent wanderings.

A fortnight after the release, the second elderly female was seen to be limping, and suffering from an open sore on her back. She was recaptured, but while she was immobilised she succumbed to one of the risks of the procedure, lying in such a way as to damage a nerve in her leg. The leg was paralysed, and despite everything the veterinary staff could do, she died a couple of months later. The end result of the first experimental translocation into Dudhwa National Park was thus two adult males and one subadult female alive and well in the new habitat.

Sale's report, which was published in *Oryx* in April 1987, shows the enormous care that was taken before and during the Dudhwa translocation, while at the same time indicating the risks and frustrations of the task. After all the work was done, the Park still did not have a breeding group of rhinoceroses, though presumably when the young female grew up one of the males would eventually find her and mate with her.

The situation was remedied in 1985, when a deal was struck with the government of Nepal, in which 16 trained Indian elephants were exchanged for four young adult female rhinoceroses captured outside Royal Chitwan National Park. The young females would not only increase the breeding potential of the Dudhwa nucleus, but would also introduce a new genetic strain, improving the vigour of the forthcoming population. One of them escaped from the holding stockade into the fenced area during her first night of captivity, and the others were released a week later. The Dudhwa population now consists of at least two breeding pairs, with the possibility that the other two adult females, soon to become three when the subadult reaches maturity, will meet and mate with one or other of the males as well. Even if this does not happen immediately, they will provide suitable 'aunts' for the offspring of the other pairs when they leave their mothers. In December 1986, all the seven surviving translocated rhinoceroses in Dudhwa were alive and well.

Conservation of Javan and Sumatran Rhinoceroses

There is very little to add about the conservation of the other two species of Asian rhinoceros. The Javan survives in Udjung Kulon, its numbers virtually unchanged for 20 years. There has been talk of moving part of the population to a small island near the present reserve, to protect the species further against poaching. The Sumatran may yet become the subject of a captive breeding operation centred around the Tabin reserve in Sabah, with the animals produced being introduced to areas of forest where the species occurred in the past. The discovery that it should be able to survive in commercial forests, providing the logging is selective, removes a major obstacle to the idea of captive propagation, which was that there would be nowhere to put the animals which were produced. However, the danger of poaching remains.

Poaching and Logging

The principal hope for the conservation of all the Asian species, the Indian included, is to remove rhinoceros horn from the Eastern pharmacopoeia. This is a slow and gradual process, but through the work of Dr Esmond Bradley Martin and others progress is being made. When it is replaced by saiga antelope horn, for example, there will be no market for the poachers, and the reason for poaching will disappear.

The same cannot be said of commercial logging, while the demand exists for precious woods from Eastern forests. Such few rhinoceroses as still exist outside declared reserves have little chance of survival, as logging creeps inexorably across their habitat. The continual losses of tropical forests have been documented elsewhere; the Asian rhinoceroses are only three of millions of species of plants as well as animals, most of them still undescribed by science, which will be lost when the forests are gone. We may have to settle for protecting them only in wildlife reserves, which in years to come may well resemble nothing more than giant zoos.

13
A Look Ahead

There are other views about the future of rhinoceroses which make more cheerful reading. Ron Thomson's picture of a time when rural Africans see the value of protecting the rhinoceroses around them, and benefit materially from their continued existence, is not the only one. David Western, formerly Chairman of the IUCN/SSC African Elephant and Rhino Specialist Group, has developed the idea of conservation outside parks, by 'finding a place for nature within the human realm'.

The World Conservation Strategy stressed the need for sustainable development. This is not a new idea (in the old days it was called 'good husbandry'), except, as Western says, to a generation brought up to regard nature reserves as 'the holy grail of conservation'. He suggests that the idea of buffer zones could be extended until they effectively cover the whole country, leaving the parks as protected centres from which the rest of the area will be restocked by natural expansion. There is no place for large wild animals in cities, but Western argues that in the rural agricultural communities which make up most of the land surface of every country there is no reason why wildlife and cultivation should not coexist.

An important requirement for this style of coexistence is political stability, allied with education and national wealth. Elephants increase their populations by an average of 2.5 per cent per year in African countries with stable governments, but they decrease by 16 per cent where the government is unstable. Although the more developed countries lost more of their elephants during their early history, they are preserving them better now. The white rhinoceros in South Africa has followed a similar course: the black in all southern African countries should recover in the same way, once the market for its horn has collapsed. Literacy and the amount of money available for conservation are the two main factors involved.

The importance of stable government in conservation was seen in Nepal, where the populations of rhinoceroses and other wildlife suffered severely during the political upheavals of the 1950s, only to recover once stability returned.

Sustainable exploitation was the hallmark of traditional hunting, which made good use of the game which was available, taking as much as was needed and conserving the rest. Some of the restraints, to be fair, were imposed by the primitive nature of the weapons available, but many were based on long experience of the growth and recovery of prey populations, with regulations expressed in the form of taboos.

Rural Africans do not now eat the rhinoceroses which they kill, although those whom Selous met during his hunting expeditions at the end of the nineteenth century were glad to be given the meat of the animals which he shot. They probably killed very few for themselves, being surrounded by other game animals which were easier to hunt. The rhinoceros meat offered to them by Selous might have been accepted as a novelty, or out of common politeness. It is quite likely that they had no traditional taboos to control the rate at which they killed rhinoceroses. Thus, when the market in horn took off, there was nothing to prevent their shooting every rhinoceros they could find: as Thomson remarks, they were probably glad to see the back of them. An untrustworthy beast in the bush, the black rhinoceros must be an uncomfortable neighbour to pastoralist and hunter alike. In the absence of traditional restraints on the killing of rhinoceroses, some new form of control is needed, one which is accepted by those people who are nearest to the animals in the field.

Western points out that commercial ranches in South Africa which combine beef production with the utilisation of wildlife increase their income by as much as 30 per cent. Other species of wildlife can be accommodated on ranches if they do not compete with domestic stock, or if they are too rare or retiring to be worth the trouble of eliminating; and others will be able to find a home in areas of the ranch which are not used by the rancher for any of a number of reasons. There are even some species which improve the ranch, either by conserving grassland, as elephants do, or by providing pleasure to the rancher. All these arguments support the idea of conserving wildlife outside parks, in harmony with agriculture. Rhinoceroses will fit in towards the end of the list.

However, Western's arguments do not cover the case of the pastoralist or the agricultural villager, disturbed by the presence of potentially dangerous animals in the bush through which he must travel, or fighting to keep wildlife out of his crops. If he is to be invited to share his habitat with black rhinoceroses, rather than killing what he can, and being kept away from the rest at gunpoint, the villager must be encouraged to develop a different attitude to them. Thomson suggests that the animals should be given a commercial value to the people who share the land with them, so that they are a source of income, either from hunting or tourism, or indeed by controlled exploitation by the people themselves. This is a point taken up by Western as well, when he asks two questions: 'How can education . . . widen the conservation support for wildlife?', and 'How can one ensure that local populations benefit preferentially from wildlife returns?'

He does not answer the questions himself, having posed them as examples of the type of question which will have to be asked and answered before his out-of-park conservation becomes a reality.

The questions are to be answered by Asian and African governments, individually and collectively, and there is very little that Westerners can do to influence them. We are in too exposed a position ourselves, having altered our own countries beyond redemption by centuries of agriculture. In Britain, this had

Plate 17 : The Javan rhinoceros survives only here, in Udjung Kulon National Park, an area which was depopulated by the eruption of Krakatoa in 1883. The population of Javan rhinos remains steady at a little over fifty animals.

Plate 18: The Sumatran rhinoceros population is the least known of all five species. Its numbers may be more than 900 or fewer than 500 in the three countries where it is believed to survive.

Plate 19: The Sumatran was the first rhinoceros to breed in captivity. This specimen is in Melaka Zoo, Malaysia.

happened before conservation meant anything other than Normans arresting Saxons for poaching their deer. We might encourage other governments not to repeat our mistakes; always a weak form of advice, especially from those who appear to have prospered as a result of their avowed errors. We might call on countries to preserve their remaining wilderness as part of the world heritage, not just for their own people's sake. Tanzania is one country which has set aside a quarter of its land explicitly as a reserve for the edification of future generations. To avoid the use of the word 'aesthetics', which can be made to sound soft and self-indulgent, one might speak of the historic and educational value of such a gesture. There are many in Britain who would dearly like to have seen preserved a large expanse of the oak and ash woodland which once covered a great part of the country.

As has been pointed out, advice of this kind might be offered by a European or any other developed country to an Asian or African country, in the confidence that if the recipient of the advice does not like it, he is free to ignore it. However, once the country has accepted the advice, its government has the problem of providing its own people with answers to Western's questions.

Where there is a conflict between agriculture and wildlife, the conservation of the wildlife will involve costs to the agriculturalists, in the form of crop damage, restrictions to their living space, or actual danger from the animals, to stock or people or both. If they are to bear these costs, they will have to be shown a compensating benefit. The historic education of their descendants might not be enough. They might explain that if the wildlife destroys their crops, displaces their stock, and kills their children, they may well not have descendants. They could be offered a share in the financial rewards which will accrue to their country, from tourism or big game hunting, as an incentive to leave the game alone. This might still not fill the bill, though if the profits were distributed locally enough, to those who were bearing the brunt of the costs, it would be a more attractive proposition.

A stronger argument, and one which is illustrated by numerous examples up and down Africa especially, is that preserving the ecosystem as a whole, in all its diversity, is a means of preserving the resilience of the environment. Sustainable use of forests and grasslands implies that enough of the original is left to regenerate itself. The complexity of ecosystems is such that no one can be sure what role any one of their components might be playing: the proper course is, therefore, to protect the whole, rhinoceroses and all.

Any of these arguments must be supportable in the face of rapidly growing human populations, whose demands for space are hard for a government to ignore. If Western's vision of a complete interdigitation between wildlife and people is to become reality, the first problem to be attacked must surely be that of excessive population growth. Without population control, the conservation of the five remaining species of rhinoceros will be achieved only by armed force, by such governments as can direct their people's activities at the point of a gun, and then only up until the time when the governments are overthrown. Translocation of breeding groups, the destruction of markets for poached products, and all the electric fences in the world will not stop hungry people from taking over the last vestige of wilderness, once their numbers have overwhelmed the land outside the reserves.

Epilogue

Especially in Africa, the fortunes of rhinoceros populations are changing fast. Efforts for their conservation will have to move equally quickly if the tide of destruction is to be stemmed. Since the bulk of this book went to press, the reported populations of the African species have changed, and the urgent work on the conservation of the black rhinoceros has begun to show results. Dr Esmond Bradley Martin and Lucy Vigne have made considerable progress in their efforts to stop the trade in rhinoceros products, with the support of conservation bodies all over the world.

The latest estimates of rhinoceros populations vary quite widely, reflecting the difficulty of counting scarce animals in large tracts of rough country. When I spoke to Dr Nigel Leader-Williams, of the Large Animal Research Unit at Cambridge University, he pointed out that accurate counting of black rhinoceroses in particular was practically impossible, even when there were as many as 4,000 in the Luangwa Valley. They live in dense bush, in rugged country, scattered over an area the size of Wales. As he put it: 'It's not like counting sparrows in an acre of woodland'.

The animals are hard to find from the air, and the terrain is too rough and far too large to search in detail on the ground. Regular patrols cover a substantial part of the Park, revisiting areas at unpredictable intervals, but their chances of catching poachers in the act are slim indeed. When they find the corpses of poached animals, it is usually long after the event, and by chance rather than as the result of a deliberate search.

With all these limitations on their accuracy, and assuming that they are carried out in a similar way, the population estimates are more valuable as indicators of change rather than as actual head counts. The extent of the change is all too clearly visible in the estimates of black rhinoceros populations over the years.

William Travers, of the Zoo Check Charitable Trust, gave me a series of figures from his 'Zoo Check' files which show the extent of the decline. In 1984, the total population of black rhinoceroses was given by IUCN as 8,400. In 1986, according to Rob Brett, of the Institute of Zoology, it was 4,500. This represents a decline of

46 per cent in two years. The figures for some individual countries are even more shocking. Count Maurice Coreth, chairman of Rhino Rescue, the Kenya-based organisation, estimated that in 1970 Kenya had 19,000 black rhinoceroses. By April 1986 his estimate was just 425, and in 1987 it had fallen below 400. Kenya has lost 98 per cent of her black rhinoceroses in less than 17 years. If the rate of loss has fallen in more recent years, it is because the animals are more difficult to find, and no doubt because some of the survivors are too closely guarded for the poachers to kill.

Bill Barclay, of the Zambian Wildlife Society, reports similar figures, saying that the Zambian population now, in 1987, is below 200. Travers' file is still open, no doubt to receive progressively more gloomy figures as the years go by.

Jane Thornbeck works for the Conservation Monitoring Centre of IUCN, publishers of the Red Data Books, maintaining the most up-to-date figures for the populations of all endangered species. She told me that after the May 1987 meeting of the African Rhino Specialist Group, the official estimate for the total black rhinoceros population was 3,832. From Leader-Williams' remarks above, the odd 32 may be taken with a pinch of salt; but whether or not they were actually counted (and whether or not they are still alive as you read this), the surviving population has fallen by 15 per cent in one year.

For the white rhinoceros, the news is mixed. The southern race, which was so recently brought back from the brink of extinction, has increased in numbers from 3,920 in 1984 to over 4,600 in 1987, a rise of about 18 per cent in three years. This may well be connected with the fact that of a total expenditure on conservation in Africa of US$160 million, South Africa spends $85 million. The estimates of the elephant population of the Luangwa Valley are significant here, as well; from a total of over 110,000 in 1973, it had fallen to 20,000 or less by March 1987, moving in parallel to the abrupt decline in black rhinoceroses, also poached to the brink of destruction. There are only two countries where the elephant population is increasing; Zimbabwe and South Africa.

The northern race of the white rhinoceros now survives only in Zaire's Garamba National Park, where in the 1970s there were 400 animals. The current population is estimated at 18 individuals, possibly as many as 20, but no more. The losses to the northern race, once a thriving reservoir of the species, have been entirely due to poaching for the dagger-handle trade in North Yemen.

The populations of the three Asian species have not been recounted since 1986, when the Indian rhinoceros was considered to be just four animals below its 1985 level; in other words, unchanged. However, the numbers do not tell the whole story. The rhinoceros population of Chitwan, in Nepal, has been increasing steadily for 13 years, by about five animals every year. If the total has remained unchanged, it follows that animals are being lost somewhere else in the species' range. Poaching is so rare in Nepal as to be negligible; the losses are from the population in India, where the inflated prices paid for Asian horn for the Chinese medical market have been sufficient to maintain the poaching pressure.

Attacking the Markets

The Chinese medical profession and the North Yemeni dagger-handle trade are two separate threats, to the Asian and African rhinoceroses respectively, but they can both be countered by attacking the market which finances the poachers. In their efforts to close down both markets, Martin and Vigne have met with notable success. In the medical market, one eastern government after another has banned the import of rhinoceros products, especially horn; Singapore and Taiwan, both major consumers and important trading centres until very recently, are among the latest. The trend is in the right direction, although too many countries modify their import bans with permission to trade in existing stocks, offering an obvious loophole for smugglers, and an incentive to corruption in the Customs House. Dr Martin's next project is to repeat his earlier survey of Asian countries, to find out whether demand has been maintained in the absence of a legitimate supply, or whether falling or stable prices indicate that the trade is indeed coming to an end. As the sources of medical horn dry up, a major media campaign is already under way to promote the acceptance of substitutes such as saiga antelope horn.

The government of North Yemen made a huge leap forward early in 1987, as described in Chapter 10, altering the pattern of trade substantially in the first six months of the year. It is too late to save the wild population of the northern race of the white rhinoceros, and so far there seems to be no diminution in the 'Rhino Wars' across the Zambesi, but it cannot be long before the demand slackens, and the poachers find that the risks which they run are not justified by their dwindling rewards.

Protection

The urgent need for protection of the black rhinoceros has led to schemes in more than one African country. In South Africa, a new National Park has been proclaimed near Barkly West, to be called Vaalbos National Park. It consists of 20,000 hectares of prime cattle ranch, with a healthy game population and plenty of good rhinoceros habitat, into which black rhinoceroses are to be introduced.

In Kenya, Zoo Check Charitable Trust, in conjunction with the Eden Trust, have enclosed 16 sq km within Tsavo National Park, containing eight black rhinoceroses. Others are to be added to the population as and when they can be captured from less well-protected areas. The target is 30 animals, and the area is to be extended as the population grows, aiming to accommodate one animal per sq km. A baby black rhinoceros which was rescued from poachers after its mother had been shot is at present being reared in captivity by Mrs Daphne Sheldrick, who has been stepmother to so many other orphans in the Tsavo area. It, too, will join the growing herd when it is old enough to look after itself.

The Rhino Rescue Trust's sanctuary at Nakuru has already been mentioned; it is another example of the last-ditch measures which are being adopted in the short term, to save some animals against the day when poaching comes to an end, and they can be released into parks which are once more safe for their kind. An undisturbed population of 60 black rhinoceroses is currently being studied by Dr Rob Brett at Ol Ari Ranch in northern Kenya, though the thickness of the bush and the timidity of the animals make his work slow and frustrating, dependent more on finding footprints and analysing urine samples than any more immediate contact with the rhinoceroses.

Ian Parker, who wrote a controversial book in 1983 called *Ivory Crisis*, concluded that it was sad but inevitable that the elephant population should be allowed to fall until it became stable 'at a level which only the African people, who have to share their land with elephants, can determine'. Another biologist, Ian Redmond, echoed his views, concluding sadly that Africa will eventually become 'a cultivated continent with a few thousand elephants kept in a handful of highly managed parks that are little more than game ranches'. These are gloomy views indeed, especially when we consider that over most of Africa the plight of the rhinoceroses is far worse than that of the elephants.

A generation of people will one day arise, none of whom will ever see a wild rhinoceros. That is inevitable, but there is no reason not to try to postpone the inevitable for as long as is rhinocerinely and humanly possible, for the sake both of the animals and ourselves.

Addresses

Here are the addresses of four organisations which collect and distribute money in the cause of rhinoceros conservation. Each is as worthy as the next of the support of those with money to spare for this urgent cause.

RHINO RESCUE TRUST at one of these two addresses:

Appeals Office
The Coach House
Grove Park
Yoxford
Suffolk IP17 3HX
England

PO Box 44597
Nairobi
Kenya

ZOO CHECK CHARITABLE TRUST

Cherry Tree Cottage
Coldharbour
Dorking
Surrey RH5 6HA
England

SAVE THE RHINO care of one of these three addresses:

East African Wildlife
  Society
PO Box 20110
Nairobi
Kenya

WWF
Avenue de Mont Blanc
CH 1196 Gland
Switzerland

World Society for the
  Protection of Animals
106 Jermyn Street
London SW1Y 6EE
England

THE DAVID SHELDRICK WILDLIFE APPEAL
PO Box 15555
Nairobi
Kenya

Select Bibliography

Animal Life Encyclopaedia vol 13 (1972), B. Grzimek (ed.), Van Nostrand Reinhold, NY

Clarke, T. H. (1986) *The Rhinoceros from Dürer to Stubbs 1515–1799*, Sotheby's, London

Encyclopaedia of Mammals vol 2 (1985), Macdonald, D. (ed.), Guild, London

Fayein, Claudie (1957) *A French Doctor in Yemen*, Robert Hale, London

Guggisberg, C. A. W. (1966) *S.O.S. Rhino*, Andre Deutsch, London

Grzimek, B. (1964) *Rhinos Belong to Everybody*, Collins, London

Grzimek, B. (1970) *Among Animals of Africa*, Collins, London

Kingdon, Jonathan (1979) *East African Mammals* vol IIIB, Academic Press, London

Martin, Esmond Bradley (1983) *Rhino Exploitation*, WWF, Hong Kong

Thomson, R. (1986) *On Wildlife 'Conservation''*, United Publishers International, NY

For current information on the status of rhinoceros populations and research, the best source is 'Oryx', the journal of the Fauna and Flora Preservation Society. It is mailed to members of the Society; membership is available from FFPS, c/o The Zoological Society of London, Regent's Park, London NW1 4RY. For American subscribers, the cost of $25.00 per year is tax-deductible.

The WWF Conservation Yearbook details all current conservation efforts including those concerned with rhinoceroses, and the 'Traffic Bulletin' from IUCN follows developments in international trade in endangered species.

Index